OSPREY COMBAT AIRCRAFT • 16

TBF/TBM
AVENGER UNITS
OF WORLD WAR 2

SERIES EDITOR: TONY HOLMES

OSPREY COMBAT AIRCRAFT • 16

TBF/TBM AVENGER UNITS
OF WORLD WAR 2

Barrett Tillman

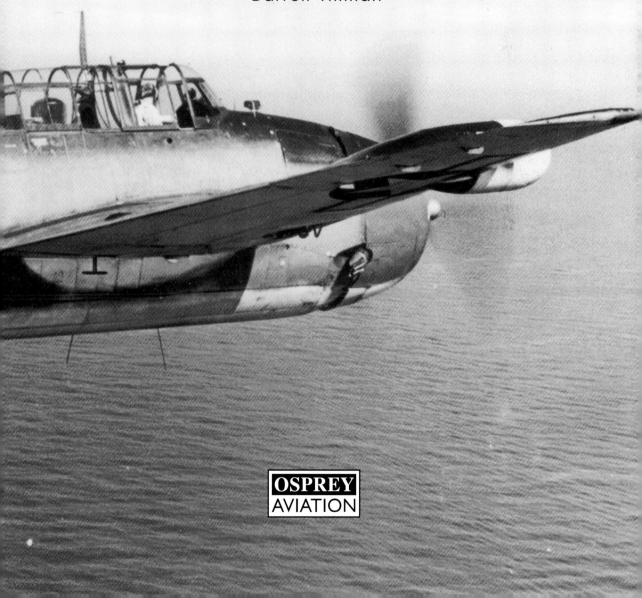

OSPREY AVIATION

Front cover
The Avenger's contribution in helping bridge the 'Atlantic Gap' has long been overshadowed by the part the aircraft played in helping secure the defeat of the Imperial Japanese Army and Navy in the Pacific. Therefore, rather than depict an AirPac TBF/TBM on the cover of this volume, we have chosen to honour the countless unsung naval aviators who spent myriad hours patrolling the cold grey waters of the northern Atlantic, searching for a most elusive foe – the German U-boat. This specially commissioned artwork by Iain Wyllie shows a TBF-1 attacking a Type VII/41 U-boat in early 1944. The aircraft is finished in the distinctive 'Atlantic ASW scheme No 2', which was comprised of dark gull grey upper surfaces and white undersides, with individual aircraft markings applied in black

Title page spread photo
Rare in the US Pacific Fleet in July 1944 was the TBM-1D with wing-mounted radar pod. This aircraft was assigned to Lt Cdr D J Melvin, commanding officer of VT-51 aboard the *Independence* class light carrier *San Jacinto*. The squadron remained aboard 'The Flagship of the Texas Navy' until late November of that year (*Author's collection*)

First published in Great Britain in 1999 by Osprey Publishing, Elms Court, Chapel Way, Botley, Oxford, OX2 9LP

ISBN 1 85532 902 6

Edited by Tony Holmes
Page design by TT Designs, T & B Truscott
Cover Artwork by Iain Wyllie
Aircraft Profiles by Tom Tullis
Scale Drawings by Mark Styling

Origination by Grasmere Digital Imaging, Leeds, UK
Printed in Hong Kong

00 01 02 03   10 9 8 7 6 5 4 3 2

ACKNOWLEDGEMENTS
Departed friends: the late Ralph Clark, Robert L Hall, Charles E Henderson III, Capt Edward J Huxtable, Rear Adm Maxwell F Leslie, Vice Adm William I Martin and Rear Adm Henry A Suerstedt. Also Capt William B Chace, Larry Coté, Capt Larry C French, Robert R Jones, Warren Omark, Tony Potachniak, H J Schonenberg, Capt Benjamin C Tate, Jim Sawruk and Charles Westbrook. The editor acknowledges the provision of photographs from the collections of Philip Jarrett, Norman Polmar and Bruce Robertson.

EDITOR'S NOTE
To make this best-selling series as authoritative as possible, the editor would be extremely interested in hearing from any individual who may have relevant photographs, documentation or first-hand experiences relating to the pilots, and their aircraft, of the various theatres of war. Any material used will be fully credited to its original source. Please write to Tony Holmes at 10 Prospect Road, Sevenoaks, Kent, TN13 3UA, Great Britain, or e-mail tony.holmes@osprey-jets. freeserve.co.uk.

CONTENTS

AVENGER

The most widely-produced naval strike aircraft of all time, the Grumman/Eastern TBF/TBM Avenger dominated the torpedo bomber role as no other American aircraft dominated any other military mission. Nearly 10,000 Avengers were produced by the parent company and Eastern Division of General Motors Corp between 1942 and 1945, supplying allied navies and air forces as well.

When it joined the fleet in early 1942, the TBF-1 Avenger was desperately needed. Its predecessor, the Douglas TBD-1 Devastator of 1937, had been procured in numbers far too small to meet wartime requirements of a two-ocean navy. Additionally, operational and combat attrition had reduced the TBD inventory from 130 airframes to about 40 by early June 1942.

Recognising the potential shortcomings of the TBD, the US Navy Bureau of Aeronautics announced a requirement for a newer, more capable, carrier-based torpedo aircraft in 1939. Design criteria included a top speed of 300 mph (260 knots), an internal bomb bay, a 3000-statute mile scouting range, and a powered turret in addition to forward- and aft-firing machine guns.

Grumman and Vought both responded with proposals, the XTBF-1 and XTBU-1, respectively. In some ways the two aircraft were well matched, but the Grumman design proved lighter and faster, with greater range, while occupying less flightdeck space than the Vought. Using the same wing-folding design later employed in the F4F-4 Wildcat and F6F-3/5 Hellcat, the TBF's span could be reduced from 54 ft 2 in to merely 18 ft 4 in. Additionally, Grumman designed a practicable, electrically-operated, turret. Although the TBU was later produced in small numbers as the Consolidated TBY Seawolf, Leroy Grumman's firm won the major contract. The Navy ordered 286 production aircraft in December 1940, powered by the Wright R-2600-8 air-cooled radial engine, rated at 1700 horsepower.

Predecessor of the Grumman Avenger was the Douglas Devastator. When it joined the fleet in 1937, the TBD-1 was an innovative aircraft: the US Navy's first carrier-based monoplane, it was of all-metal construction, with power folding wings and semi-retractable landing gear. Of 130 procured, 100 remained at the time of Pearl Harbor, and only a handful survived the Battle of Midway in June 1942 (*Peter M Bowers*)

Grumman's mock-up of the XTBF-1 in original form, without the dorsal fillet ahead of the vertical fin. The first prototype is thought to have flown once or twice without the fillet, which became standard on all subsequent Avengers to enhance stability (*Grumman*)

A 'family portrait' of the TBF mock-up alongside the fuselage of the 50th F4F-3 Wildcat built by Grumman. Other than size, the torpedo bomber was far more complex than the fighter, with power folding wings, hydraulically-operated landing gear, an electrically-powered turret and, of course, an internal bomb bay (*Grumman*)

Inevitably, there were complications. For example, the 'X job's' anticipated 320-mph top speed was reduced to 275 owing to weight increases and centre of gravity problems. However, Grumman test pilot Robert L Hall made the first flight in the XTBF-1 (BuNo 2539) on 7 August 1941. Exactly one year later, Avengers would provide carrier-based air support for the marine landings at Guadalcanal.

Hall's account of the flight was professionally concise;

'This first flight lasted but five minutes and was really only a high-speed taxy test with a short lift-off. The second flight of the day was 10 minutes, and the third the following day lasted 41 minutes.

'During the rest of August and through September and October I flew this same airplane 20 times for a total of 23 hours. I did not fly a TBF again until February 1942, when I did the dive demonstrations at Anacostia and Dahlgren, Maryland.'

On 28 November 1941, BuNo 2539 was destroyed on a routine test flight. Test pilot Hobart Cook and engineer Gordon Israel were air-borne when a leak in the 1500-psi hydraulic system filled the cockpit with a fine mist that was mistaken for smoke. Cook reported an in-flight fire, then bailed out with Israel 15 miles from the factory field at Bethpage, Long Island. Cook alit safely, but Israel broke an ankle on a telephone pole. The aircraft crashed near Brentwood, New York.

Loss of the prototype could have been a severe setback. However, the navy had approved construction of a second XTBF-1, and Grumman had nearly completed the fuselage. The second aircraft was finished in only three weeks, successfully flying on 15 December 1941.

By then, of course, the need was more urgent than ever.

That winter, a joint army/navy aviation board began assigning popular names to military aircraft. According to company legend, the TBF project engineer, Raymond Koch, wanted to christen his torpedo bomber the 'Revenger' in the wake of Pearl Harbor. Whatever the background of the name, the TBF became the 'Avenger' instead.

Production of TBF-1s began slowly. The first was delivered in January 1942, and five more followed in February. Torpedo Squadron 8, assigned to the new carrier *Hornet*, received the first TBF-1s while still in training at NAS Norfolk, Virginia. However, further delay was incurred in March when the first half-dozen aircraft were returned to the factory for replacement wing-fold hinge pins.

By June 1942 – at the time of the Battle of Midway – Grumman was producing 60 TBFs per month, and exceeded 100 in November. The first year's production totalled 646, and during 1943 Grumman maintained an average of nearly 150 per month. But the F6F Hellcat had priority among all Grumman designs, and in early 1942 arrangements were made for Eastern Aircraft Division of General Motors to begin building Avengers as TBM-1s at Trenton, New Jersey.

Production variants differed relatively little throughout the war. The TBF-1C incorporated a .50-cal machine gun in each wing to augment the pilot's .30-cal gun firing through the propeller arc. The XTBF-2 proved a dead end with its two-stage supercharged engine, although

Pilots of Torpedo Squadron 8 inspect one of the first TBF-1s delivered to NAS Norfolk in January/February 1942. This excellent elevated view clearly shows off the bombardier's position behind the pilot. The second cockpit also had flight controls, which were deleted as unnecessary after the 50th production aircraft. Although US Navy and Marine Corps squadrons almost never flew with this position occupied, it was generally standard in the Royal Navy, with the addition of an observer to the flightcrew. Many early Avengers were returned to the factory for modifications to improve functioning of the wing folding mechanisms, thus preventing scheduled deployment to the Pacific aboard the carrier USS *Hornet* (CV 8) (*Grumman*)

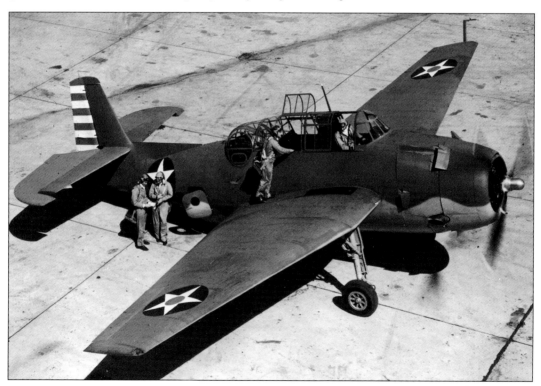

the -3 model produced by Eastern gained 100 horsepower in the R-2600-20 engine, surface search radar and underwing rocket rails. A distinctive recognition feature on late-model TBM-3s was the externally-mounted tailhook.

Despite sometimes warranted concern of the automotive industry's ability to mass-produce aircraft to aviation tolerances, Eastern proved its worth. Its extensive experience in production techniques, combined with Grumman's methods of simplifying assembly, made a winning team. The first TBMs were actually GM-assembled aircraft from Grumman parts, with one being completed in November and two in December 1942. Thirty-one were built in the first three months of 1943, after which GM production grew in astonishing leaps. TBM deliveries accelerated to a plateau of 100 in July, attaining that level somewhat faster than Grumman itself. The last TBFs were delivered in December 1943, for a total of 2291.

Throughout 1944, Eastern Aircraft built an average of nearly ten TBMs per day, with monthly production reaching a record high of 400 in March 1945. Japan's rapid capitulation in mid-August resulted in an almost immediate end to Avenger production, with 328 accepted that month. The last 24 TBMs were delivered in September 1945, for an Eastern total of 7546. Annual breakdowns included:

The first production TBF-1 (BuNo 00373) is seen in flight on 23 March 1942 in the landing configuration: 'Wheels down, flaps down, hook down'. Note how the tailwheel prevents the radioman from using his .30-cal machine gun – a problem occasionally encountered in combat when battle damage released hydraulic pressure and the wheel dropped into the extended position (*Grumman*)

Year	TBFs	TBMs	Total
1942	646	3	649
1943	1645	1109	2754
1944	—	3481	3481
1945	—	2953	2953
Totals	**2291**	**7546**	**9837**

INTO SERVICE

Torpedo Squadron 8 at Norfolk, Virginia, took delivery of the first fleet Avengers in April 1942. At the end of May the navy had 84 TBF-1s, including 32 assigned to the AirPac pool in San Diego, with 21 assigned to VT-8 in Hawaii. The numbers grew steadily thereafter – 140 on hand in June, with five fleet squadrons holding from five to 17 aircraft, not counting *Lexington's* VT-2, which was soon disestablished following the ship's loss at Coral Sea.

By 27 August – three weeks after the Guadalcanal landings – BuAer had had 268 TBF-1s transferred from the East Coast of the USA to carriers operating in the Solomons. *Saratoga, Enterprise, Hornet* and *Wasp* all embarked Avengers, although the location and allowance list shows two TBD-1s sharing deck space with VT-7's TBFs in *Wasp*. Additionally, two replacement air groups on the West Coast also had Avengers, namely VT-11 at San Diego and VT-12 at Alameda.

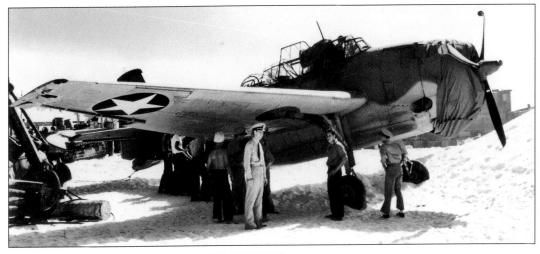

SUPPORTING THE PRODUCT

Getting torpedo bombers to the fleet was one thing; keeping them flying was another. Grumman established a skilled team of civilian technical representatives to work with navy squadrons around the globe. One of the best-known 'tech reps' was a 22-year-old New Yorker by the name of Ralph Clark. He went directly to work at Grumman after graduating from college in May 1941 and, although initially concerned exclusively with the complex power turret, he was soon made responsible for the whole TBF 'tech rep' programme.

'I became involved in the whole aeroplane almost immediately. The oil system, the hydraulics, you name it. The single biggest problem we had was the hydraulics. Previously, our aeroplanes mainly had vacuum flaps, mechanical flaps or, as in the F4F, mechanical cranking of the landing gear. Also manual folding of the wings, so everything before the TBF had been vacuum or manual. We now moved into completely hydraulic operations, which was a whole new field.

'I had an "instant Avenger repair kit" in the trunk of my car in Hawaii. Using small envelopes of hydraulic seals, I was able to nearly double the number of airworthy aeroplanes by just supplying the right

The only survivor of six VT-8 Avengers deployed to Midway Atoll for the June 1942 battle was 8-T-1, flown by Ens Albert K Earnest. Lt L K Fieberling led the Torpedo Eight detachment against the Japanese carriers, but lacking fighter support, five were shot down. With his gunner dead, his radioman wounded and himself injured, Earnest brought his battered BuNo 00380 back to Midway for a one-wheel landing. 8-T-1 is seen here draped with engine and cockpit covers, having been jacked up and placed on both main mounts. Battle damage to the starboard wingtip is clearly visible. Ens Earnest received the unique distinction of being awarded two Navy Crosses for his Midway mission: one for attacking the Japanese fleet and the other for his return to base (*National Archives*)

The turret of Earnest's Avenger bears mute testimony to damage inflicted by A6M2 Zero fighters. The gunner, Seaman 1st Class J D Manning, died from wounds sustained while firing at enemy interceptors in the low-level combat as VT-8 approached the Japanese fleet (*National Archives*)

seal at the right time. For some reason, the navy had not got a large enough supply of the right seals out to the fleet. A mechanic would put in a request for the particular seal and would get back a slip marked "NIS" – "not in stock". They hadn't got that far in the supply system yet.

'So Grumman would mail me the envelopes of seals after I told them what was needed. And with a big brown envelope filled with various seals, we were able to put up additional aeroplanes almost daily. It was a major breakthrough just to have enough hydraulic seals available.

'We occasionally had a structural problem, but not very many. I don't recall much trouble with the wing folding mechanism. The legend is that Mr Grumman designed that system using a rubber eraser and a paperclip he'd bent out of shape. This was for the Wildcat, but the same principle applied to our other aeroplanes.

'I do remember one problem when we were shifting Avenger production to General Motors for the TBM. The navy had developed glide bombing, in which they approached a target at 50 degrees instead of the 70 degrees they used for the SBDs. Theoretically, this 50-degree glide was to be used by TBFs when torpedoes weren't reliable enough and bombs were used.

'I rode with Bill Martin and some of his boys in VT-10, and they were half-crazy. The aeroplane was supposed to be redlined at 315 knots (370 mph) in a dive, but they were getting up to 370 knots (425 mph). It worked most of the time in TBFs, but some of the early TBMs had trouble. A couple of aeroplanes ripped their wings off. I was back in the states, working at NAS Jacksonville, Florida, which had TBFs. At nearby Fort Lauderdale, they had TBMs. Their skipper was Cdr Joe Taylor, who had led VT-5 from the old *Yorktown* in the Coral Sea. Joe got hold of me and said two of his TBMs had pulled their wings off while glide bombing and the crews were killed.

'Finally, we found a TBM which had a partially bent wing. It was just what we were looking for, since the wing hadn't failed, but it showed us where it was overstressed. We took that wing off the aeroplane and sent it to Grumman. The factory took the wing apart and analysed it. They found that the rivet pattern had been changed at GM for production purposes. As a result, it had

A six-aeroplane division of TBFs undertakes a training mission over the Florida Everglades in 1942. The usual tactical organisation at this time was two three-aeroplane sections in each division, with three divisions for a total of 18 aircraft per squadron. However, unit-strength combat missions were extremely rare owing to the need for simultaneous scouting and attack, as well as the inevitable aircraft down for maintenance (*Grumman*)

lost some of the original strength. Naturally, the necessary changes were made on Eastern's production line. But other than that, they did a great job. They even had their own service department with their own "tech reps", so I think they did a good job.

'At the time of the Battle of Midway, near the first weekend in June 1942, Grumman's general manager Jake Swirbul made a speech. That Friday he got everybody together on the apron in back of the plant and stood up on a work bench with a microphone. He said, "There's a big battle going on out there, and the navy's in trouble. We have to give them every aeroplane we can by Monday. So I want everybody in the place to work until you can't work anymore". We turned on and took every spare part we could find, everything we could put together, and on Monday morning there were 22 new aeroplanes sitting out on the line. All different types, but mostly F4Fs and TBFs.'

<u>MIDWAY</u>

Swirbul's speech was no mere rhetoric. Following the Coral Sea battle by four weeks, the Battle of Midway was only the second aircraft carrier engagement in history. Vice Admiral Chuichi Nagumo's carrier striking force (*Kido Butai*) was composed of four veteran 'flattops' which had attacked Pearl Harbor on 7 December. With overwhelming local superiority around Midway, the stage was set for a decisive Japanese triumph – the outnumbered US Pacific Fleet could not permit the enemy to occupy Midway Atoll, barely a thousand miles from Oahu.

With advance intelligence of Japanese plans, the Pacific Fleet scraped together all available forces. On 8 May 1942 the Torpedo 8 contingent remaining in Norfolk was directed to proceed to the West Coast for immediate transfer to Hawaii. The 19 Avengers arrived at Pearl Harbor on 29 May – less than 24 hours after *Hornet* had deployed with Commander Waldron's 15 TBDs.

Only a day later, the call went out for volunteers to ferry six Avengers to Midway, 1100 nautical miles north-west of Pearl Harbor. Lt Langdon K Fieberling was designated officer in charge of the detachment for the impending battle, and he led six TBFs into the air for the long ferry flight on the morning of 1 June. His five pilots were Ensigns C E Brannon, A K Earnest, O J Gaynier, V A Lewis, and non-commissioned aviator, D

One of the classic Avenger photos of World War 2 is this five-aeroplane echelon of TBF-1s dramatically silhouetted against a majestic backdrop of cumulus clouds. The colours and markings are typical 1942 – blue-grey upper surfaces and medium grey lower, with the national insignia in six positions, without the red centre (*Grumman*)

Naval colours in transition. Taken in May 1943, this photo depicts a VC-22 aircraft assigned to the light carrier USS *Independence* (CVL-22). An early version of the tri-colour scheme (white undersurfaces, medium blue sides and dark-blue upper) is offset with 'Stateside' unit markings and the cockade style star. Horizontal bars were added later that year (*Author's collection*)

D Woodside. Each aircraft carried a radioman and a turret gunner, with two TBFs containing designated navigators. The latter were much needed, for some of the ensigns had never been beyond sight of shore!

Eight hours after take-off, Fieberling led his flight to landings on Eastern Island, where torpedoes were loaded. After the urgency of getting TBFs to Midway, the next two days passed with almost boring routine. Then, early on the morning of the 4th, things changed.

The only Avenger pilot to survive the Battle of Midway was Ens Albert K Earnest. He submitted an after-action report later that month, which read in part;

'On the morning of 4 June, we manned our planes as usual at 0400, warmed them up, cut the engines and prepared to stand by during the morning alert. At 0545 I was told by a Marine officer to start my engine, as unknown planes had been sighted by a patrol plane 100 miles from Midway.

'At 0600 we taxied out, took off and joined up in two three-plane sections, planes and sections stepped down. We set out on a course of 320 degrees True, at an airspeed of 160 knots indicated, at an altitude of 2000 ft. Approximately five minutes after take-off we were attacked by two or three enemy planes, one of which I tentatively identified as a Messerschmitt 109 fighter. We evaded these planes, climbed to 4000 ft, and continued on our course.

'At approximately 0700 we sighted the enemy force about 15 miles away, headed for Midway Island. It was a force of about ten ships; destroyers, cruisers and at least one battleship, forming a screen around two long carriers. Just as we sighted the enemy fleet, we were attacked by a large force of enemy fighters. We immediately started a dive at full throttle through clouds to within 150 ft of the water and headed directly for the carriers. The enemy fighters, which seemed to outnumber us at least three to one, were Zero fighters and Messerschmitts. They continued to attack us, and on the second burst hit my turret gunner, AMM3/c J D Manning, putting him out of action and eventually killing him. At the same time, my hydraulic system was shot away, causing my tail wheel to drop down and blank out my tunnel gun. Soon after this my tunnel gunner, RM2/c H H Ferrier, was hit on the head, and although dazed and bleeding, was not seriously injured. I received a small cut on the right cheek, apparently by shrapnel from an explosive shell.

'When we were still several miles from the Japanese carriers, my elevator wires were shot away. I released my torpedo at the nearest ship, a light cruiser, as I thought I was out of control, but regained control with the elevator tab before hitting the water. I could not see whether or not my torpedo hit the cruiser.

'Two enemy fighters chased me for about ten minutes after this, and although they made runs on me as well, no vital parts of the plane were hit and it continued to perform very well. After the enemy planes left me, I looked back at the enemy fleet and could see no signs of any ships having been hit. I then returned to Midway and was forced to make a crash landing, since both of my wheels would not come down. None of the other TBF-1 airplanes returned to the base.'

Earnest, who had been briefed to expect carrier-based Bf 109Es in addition to A6M2 Zeros, was extraordinarily fortunate to survive the fighter attacks. He received a rare honour – perhaps unique – in being awarded two Navy Crosses for his Midway mission: one for his attack on the Japanese fleet, and the other for returning his aircraft to Eastern Island.

Fieberling's six TBFs had attacked Nagumo's carriers at about the same time as 27 Marine Corps SBDs and SB2Us and four US Army B-26s. No damage was inflicted upon the invasion fleet, which included four carriers, two battleships, three cruisers and a dozen destroyers. Japanese flak and fighters chopped the American formations to pieces, destroying 19 of the 37 land-based Dauntlesses, Vindicators, Avengers and Marauders.

However, the Midway attack groups accomplished an important goal. Nagumo was forced to manoeuvre while avoiding the mixed-service strike, and incurred further delay from the three Devastator squadrons that arrived soon thereafter. Consequently, the Zero combat air patrol was brought to low-level, leaving it completely out of position when three *Enterprise* and *Yorktown* SBD squadrons attacked *Kido Butai* with fully armed and fuelled air-craft on deck. The result was disastrous for the 'Empire of the Sun' – three carriers were destroyed out-right, and the fourth was hunted to destruction that evening.

The second USS *Yorktown* (CV 10) was named for CV 5, veteran of Coral Sea and sunk at Midway. Commissioned in 1943, she was second ship of the *Essex* class, and originally embarked Air Group Five: squadrons with the same numbers as CV 5's units. The TBF-1s arrayed forward of the island in this impressive view belong to Torpedo Five, with tricolour schemes and fairly unusual side numbers. The nearest aircraft, 5-T-15, is typical in having the aircraft number 15 rendered twice the size of the 5-T segment (*Grumman*)

GUADALCANAL AND THE SOLOMONS

The Guadalcanal campaign, which officially lasted from August 1942 until February 1943, involved TBFs in combat both afloat and ashore. Aside from carrier-based navy squadrons, the first marine torpedo bomber unit was also committed to the campaign action. Although designated a scout-bomber squadron, Lt Col Paul Moret's VMSB-131 inaugurated the Avenger to combat in time for the climax of the campaign in November 1942.

Just 17 days after the First Marine Division's landings on Guadalcanal and Tulagi, the war's third carrier battle occurred. On 24 August the two available US carriers, *Enterprise* and *Saratoga*, fought three Japanese 'flattops' in the Battle of the Eastern Solomons. At stake was continued seaborne communications to supply the marines ashore.

Embarked in *Enterprise*, Torpedo Three, led by Lt Cdr Charles M Jett, was *Saratoga's* TorpRon, which still had not rejoined its parent ship after being displaced from the sunken *Yorktown* at Midway. Similarly, 'Sara' operated *Hornet's* Torpedo Eight, under the command of Lt Cdr Harold H Larsen, better known as 'Swede'. Both units entered the Guadalcanal battle with 15 TBF-1s.

On the afternoon of the 24th, seven of Jett's aeroplanes departed *Enterprise*, searching for the reported Japanese fleet units, while *Saratoga* prepared a strike group. Each Avenger was armed with two 500-lb bombs in case contact was made with the enemy.

Jett and his wingman, Ens R J Bye, did just that. Nearly 200 miles north of their launch position, they found the 11,000-ton light carrier *Ryujo*, with three escorts. The two TBFs circled northwest of the enemy force and executed a horizontal bombing attack from upsun at 12,200 ft. There was no AA fire until the Avengers were nearly at the drop point – their four bombs landed in a cluster 500 ft astern of *Ryujo*. It was a disappointing result, but

Torpedo Eight inaugurated the Avenger to combat while flying from Midway, and subsequently took the new torpedo bomber to sea in *Saratoga*. Ens F G Marriman nosed up 'Tare 64' on 16 September 1942, resulting in damage to the propeller and possible sudden stoppage damage to the Wright R-2600 engine. However, BuNo 00421 was back on the flight schedule not long afterward (*Author's collection*)

Commanding the Enterprise Air Group during the Battle of the Eastern Solomons was Lt Cdr Maxwell F Leslie, who had previously served as CO of Bombing Three during the Battle of Midway. Leslie converted from an SBD to a TBF in his new role as 'CAG', and flew an extraordinarily long mission on the evening of 24 August, recovering aboard *Saratoga* after dark. It was no more than his fifth 'trap' in an Avenger, and his first at night! (*Author's collection*)

with the Japanese fully alerted, there was no point in staying. The VT-3 section quickly turned for home, having made the only horizontal bombing attack Avengers would ever make on an underway carrier.

In an adjoining search sector, Lt J N Myers and Machinist H L Corl sighted a Japanese cruiser. They prepared for a bomb run but were suddenly intercepted by Zeros – one passed so close that Myers could see a red stripe around the fuselage – and although the A6M2s scored no hits on the first pass, Myers and Corl were forced to break off. The cruiser was firing accurate AA bursts, and one Zero pursued Corl into a cloud. The latter was killed, but his gunner, Radioman D D Wiley, survived to return to Guadalcanal almost seven months later.

Meanwhile, Myers' TBF was badly shot up by a Zero near the American task force. The Japanese air strike, launched almost simultaneously, caught several US aircraft in the area, and Ens R J Bye of VT-3 fought an inconclusive duel with an Aichi D3A before running out of fuel. Another of Jett's Avengers also ditched, but both crews were rescued.

At 1430, more than an hour after *Enterprise's* search departed, *Saratoga* sent up 28 SBDs and eight TBFs to deal with *Ryujo*. Leading the Avengers was Lt Bruce L Harwood, who aborted with engine problems, but the other seven pressed on. One of them was Ens Bert Earnest, the only surviving TBF pilot from Torpedo Eight's six-aeroplane Midway detachment.

Upon sighting the target, the strike leader, Cdr H D Felt, directed five TBFs against the carrier and two against the cruiser *Tone*, with the Dauntlesses divided accordingly.

The big Grummans bored in at 200 ft, Lt Harwood leading three on the starboard bow and two to port. All five launched their torpedoes inside 900 yards, and one of those dropped from the starboard side scored a hit. It is possible that two more also struck, but American as well as Japanese reports were contradictory. As the TBFs pulled off target, *Ryujo* was already listing, burning badly from bomb hits and the torpedo.

Tone escaped damage from both torpedoes aimed at her, and the seven SBDs originally targeted against her were redirected to *Ryujo*. During the attack and retirement, three Avengers were holed by flak or fighters, but all returned to the task force.

Enterprise's new air group commander was Lt Cdr Maxwell F Leslie, formerly skipper of Bombing Three. He remained aboard through most of the day, co-ordinating his squadrons' strikes and searches. At around 1900 the Americans received warning of another enemy raid en route. *Enterprise* and *Saratoga* scrambled to clear their decks, lest they be caught in the same vulnerable predicament that doomed *Kido Butai* at Midway.

'Sara' launched five TBFs and two SBDs against a reported battleship and cruiser formation. Leading the mini strike was VT-8 skipper 'Swede' Larsen. Four Avengers found Japanese cruisers and launched torpedoes, but the Japanese warships escaped harm. Two of Larsen's pilots got lost in the darkening sky and ditched in the ocean.

Enterprise had launched a deckload strike of 31 aircraft, including seven TBFs. Directed to find and attack a Japanese surface unit near

A fine echelon right formation of 12 VT-10 Avengers in Southwest Pacific waters circa October 1942. The second TBF bears a white 'GC' legend forward of the fuselage star, indicating the air group commander, Richard K Gaines. Although unclear in this photograph, the TBF nearest to the camera (the CO's aircraft) was fitted with an experimental installation of externally-mounted .50-cal machine guns on the wingroots, this 'mod' being engineered by Grumman technical representative Ralph Clark in response to squadron requests for greater forward firepower. The makeshift arrangement proved functional, but was improved in TBF-1Cs, which had internally wing-mounted .50-cals to augment the original .30-cals firing through the propeller arc. During the Battle of Santa Cruz VT-10 lost six aircraft and *Hornet's* VT-6 another nine

Ryujo's reported position, the group broke up when a Japanese strike appeared. The 15 Wildcats engaged the raiders, leaving the SBDs and TBFs to fend for themselves. And fend they did, as Machinist J R Baker's gunner, ARM3/c C L Gibson, claimed an D3A 'Val' with two bursts from his .50-cal gun.

The last to launch was Lt Cdr Leslie, who recalled;

'I flew a specially configured TBF, which had extra gasoline tanks for longer duration. It was considered the ideal type for CAGs to fly because it had good armament and extra radio equipment. This was a most interesting flight for me, for several reasons. I was spotted aft for take-off because I required more run, and minutes before the take-off signal, I was told to cut my engine. I didn't know the reason, but then I heard that a Japanese attack was imminent and the ship was turning.

'After a brief interval, I was again told to start my engine and I took off. I made the usual left climbing turn, and as I looked back I saw a puff of smoke come from the aft elevator where I had been parked. I later learned that a Jap bomb had made a direct hit, with the explosion killing several people below decks, and the after elevator blown up about two feet.

'I then departed on a track to catch up with the squadrons, which were headed for what had been reported as an enemy carrier. At this instant I was approaching our AA screen of destroyers and the battleship *North Carolina*, and I happened to be looking at it when I saw several gun flashes which appeared to be shells coming in my direction. Sure enough, in another brief instant I noticed several small holes in my left wing. I dived for the water and got out of there as fast as 175 knots would take me.

'I continued on the projected heading and attempted to contact the squadrons by radio, but no luck. I went to what was undoubtedly reported as the wake of fast ships, and it turned out to be a reef with the water breaking over it. The air group had departed *Enterprise* at about 1900, and it was now just before sundown, and I visualised a difficult time locating the ship upon return well after dusk, and I was right. I never did contact my squadrons, and they had been ordered by *Enterprise* to head for and land at Guadalcanal.

'It was pitch dark when I

arrived at the supposed area for *Enterprise,* but all ships were running darkened and nothing was in sight. I then headed in what I thought was the proper course for the ships to retreat, and finally passed over one which I could only observe because of the high speed wake astern of it. I didn't know whether or not it was friendly, and they probably had the same concern about me. It was at least heading in the same direction as I, and that gave me some encouragement.

Two TBF-1s (almost certainly Marine Corps aircraft) prepare to taxy off the parking apron for a Solomon Islands mission circa 1943. The Avenger in the foreground, with its engine already running, bears the fuselage number 313, which was a Marine practise based upon the last three digits of the Bureau of Aeronautics serial number. Meanwhile, a plane captain prepares to start the other aircraft via a cartridge in the engine accessory compartment (*Grumman*)

'After another half-hour I received a plain language call over the radio saying, "Max, keep coming and gain some altitude". It was my Annapolis classmate, Ham Dow, who was the radio officer on the staff of Admiral Fletcher, and it was the best news I had ever received. In those days radar wasn't too well developed, but Ham Dow was one of the most influential in developing it, and he stayed with my blip on the screen until I arrived in the task force area.

'It was now well after 2300, the ships were darkened, and all I could see was their silhouettes on the water. I still didn't know if they were friendly or enemy. However, I then got the word via radio that the *Saratoga* would turn on all its running lights for me to land aboard. I had made but three or four carrier landings in a TBF, and never one at night, but I was more than willing to try this one. It happened to turn out well.

'All planes on deck had been spotted forward getting ready for a sunrise launch, and they had been kept there until the last minute, awaiting my arrival. I was told that in another five minutes they were going to have to be pushed aft, so that shows how narrow a margin I had.

'I will forever have a profound debt of gratitude to the magic of radar, and the persistence of Ham Dow in using it. I was quite deaf from four and three-quarter hours in the air, but after Admiral Fletcher called me up to the bridge, he told me to go down to his cabin and turn in on his brass-railed double bed.'

Thus ended the Avenger's first carrier engagement, in which VT-3 and -8 had launched 27 aircraft during four searches or strikes. Twelve TBFs had attacked Japanese ships, including the light carrier *Ryujo*, which was sunk. The seven bomb-armed Grummans obtained no hits on their targets.

Losses amounted to seven Avengers, or 26 percent of the TBFs launched on combat missions. However, only three of the losses were directly attributable to enemy action, as *Saratoga's* Torpedo Three lost two aircraft to fuel exhaustion, and jettisoned two more with heavy damage.

The Eastern Solomons battle provided the first meaningful assessment of the new torpedo aeroplane. VT-3 stated in part;

'It is considered that the TBF-1 has numerous possibilities as a combatant plane, inner and intermediate air patrol plane, and as a glide

A VT-11 TBF-1 shows battle damage upon returning to Guadalcanal during the summer of 1943. A Japanese anti-aircraft shell destroyed nearly half the port horizontal stabiliser, although it left the elevator relatively untouched. The Avenger's tough airframe endeared it to aircrews (*Author's collection*)

bomber. The possibilities of this plane are limited only by the experience and training of the individual combat crews. More armament is desirable to increase the defensive characteristics of the plane. With an increase in firepower, especially forward, this plane is considered superior in combat to Japanese dive-bombers.

'There appears to be room for improvement in communication doctrine between an air group and its carrier, and between various air groups in a task force. Should the TBF-1 be used as a scout, it could effectively home an air attack group to a located enemy force. Minor arrangements of communication facilities in this plane will allow the radioman-turret gunner to key contact reports while manning the turret.

'The TBF-1 would be more effective as a scout if it were equipped with a half-size belly tank (125-130 gallon capacity). Such an arrangement would allow the plane more endurance, and still enable it to carry two 500-lb bombs.'

SANTA CRUZ

The fourth carrier battle in less than five months occurred in late October 1942. As usual, the Americans were outnumbered while defending a crucial position – in this instance, that position still being Guadalcanal.

Enterprise and *Hornet* were the major combatants capable of defeating a combined Japanese army-navy effort to seize Guadalcanal once and for all. Powerful seaborne units screened the enemy reinforcements, and a large sea-air engagement was fought throughout 27 October. It passed into history as the Battle of Santa Cruz.

The battle went badly for the US Navy. *Hornet* was sunk, *Enterprise* was damaged and no Japanese warships were lost, but the hard-fought battle blunted Japan's penultimate drive against 'Cactus'. *Enterprise* flew the new Air Group Ten, with the TorpRon under the command of Lt Cdr John A Collett, while *Hornet* flew a mixed air group which included the 'Big E's' former VT-6, led by Lt Edwin B Parker. Between them, the two torpedo squadrons had 24 operational TBFs.

That Tuesday morning, *Enterprise* launched a hasty 20-aeroplane strike against Japanese carriers reported by scouts to be some 200 miles distant. Plans to co-ordinate with *Hornet's* air group turned to hash in the haste and confusion, so the 'Big E's' CAG, Cdr Richard Gaines, proceeded with his small formation.

Both sides launched strike groups that knew where to find the opposition. Consequently, the *Enterprise* squadrons crossed paths with the *Zuiho* fighter squadron 60 miles from the US task force. Making the attack from above and behind, Lt Saneyasu Hidaka led his nine A6M2s in a surprise interception that knocked down the lead TBF in the first pass. Lt Cdr Collett's engine was set afire and he parachuted but was never found. His radioman, ARM1/c T C Nelson, survived as a prisoner.

But the *Enterprise* men fought back. Aided by two other gunners, AM2/c R B Holmgrin in Lt(jg) Richard K Batten's aeroplane scored a spectacular kill by exploding a Zero within 100 yards of VT-10's second division.

The fight was short and violent. Two Wildcats went down and two more were forced out of the combat – the entire division on the port side of the formation. A second TBF, flown by Ens John Reed, exploded under Zero gunfire with the gunner escaping – Reed's radioman, Murray Glasser, was also rescued by a Japanese destroyer. Wildcats claimed three kills, but two other TBFs dropped out of formation. One of them downed another Mitsubishi fighter, credited to Lt Macdonald Thompson's radioman, Charles E Shinneman.

Hidaka's Zeros had torn the *Enterprise* formation apart. Three F4Fs and two TBFs were destroyed, and another Wildcat plus two Avengers aborted with battle damage. However, the *Zuiho* fighters also took heavy losses, with four being downed, plus one damaged. Hidaka ruefully abandoned his mission and led the survivors back to his ship.

Meanwhile, Cdr Richard Gaines in his unarmed TBF continued on with four remaining Avengers, the three Dauntlesses and four Wildcats. By the time the Japanese vanguard force was seen, the SBDs had drifted away from the formation, leaving Lt Thompson to attack the cruiser *Suzuya* while Lt Cdr James Flatley strafed with his F4Fs to suppress flak. It was a frustrating experience; with only two torpedoes released during the initial attack, both of which missed. The third pilot returned for another try, made a successful drop, and likewise missed. The VS-10 Dauntlesses later attacked another cruiser, *Chikuma*, and inflicted some damage.

Meanwhile, the *Hornet* SBDs found the main enemy force and savaged *Shokaku* with several bomb hits. She was out of the battle, although her air group had already found the US task force. Torpedo Six's two divisions, launched separately from *Hornet*, coincidentally attacked two cruisers shortly after the dive-bombers struck *Shokaku*. Lt E B Parker's six Avengers went after *Tone*, dropped five torpedoes (one evidently failed to release) and missed.

Lt Ward F Powell's nine bombers had bypassed the Japanese unit in search of bigger game, then returned to harry the damaged *Chikuma*. Parker took his aeroplanes into a glide bombing attack that scored at least one hit that compounded the damage inflicted by VS-10 SBDs. With aviation fuel from the cruiser's floatplane blazing topside, *Chikuma* sustained nearly 300 casualties.

A one-time fighter pilot, Lt(jg) Humphrey L Tallman, had broken off when his bombs failed to release. Dissatisfied with events, he found a light cruiser and succeeded in dropping four 500-pounders, one of which may have scored.

Hornet's TBFs had escaped without loss, but it was still a long flight home. Six Avengers ditched out of fuel, including one of two VT-10 aircraft flying with Torpedo Six. Another Avenger was lost to Japanese fighters escorting the bombers and torpedo aircraft attacking *Enterprise*

Marine TBFs at Munda airfield in October 1943. During this period both marine and navy Avengers were heavily committed to the Rabaul, New Britain, aerial offensive. Note the disparity of national insignia – only the Avenger parked in the middle distance on the left has the horizontal bars which became standard later that year (*Author's collection*)

and *Hornet*, Lt(jg) Rufus Clark last being seen by VT-6 chasing raiders through 'friendly' flak bursts. He was shot down and killed with his crew, fighting *Junyo* pilots who identified his TBF as a TBD.

Japanese numbers and persistence finally overwhelmed the hard-pressed American combat air patrol. F4F-4s ran out of ammunition and could not prevent D3A 'Val' dive-bombers and B5N 'Kate' torpedo aircraft from inflicting fatal damage upon *Hornet*. *Enterprise* was also hit and forced to withdraw.

In all, only ten torpedo-armed Avengers found any targets in the battle, and the eight 'fish' they launched all missed. Losses among 'torpeckers' were heavy – of the 29 engaged, three had been shot down and no fewer than 16 ran out of fuel or were damaged beyond repair in deck crashes. Three TBF pilots and five aircrew were killed, with two more crewmen captured.

One other torpedo needs to be accounted for. When Lt(jg) Batten ditched his Avenger following the shoot-out with *Junyo* Zeros, a bizarre event unfolded. Unable to get aboard *Enterprise*, Batten ditched almost a mile ahead of the destroyer *Porter* (DD-356), which went dead in the water to pick up the VT-10 crew. Unexpectedly, a torpedo was sighted to port, and two Wildcats attempted to detonate the threat with gunfire. However, the American Mk XIII slammed into *Porter's* beam and caused fatal damage. Later evaluation determined that Batten's weapon had become dislodged in the ditching, launched itself and made a circular run to sink the very ship rescuing the aircrew!

However, regardless of the tactical outcome of the Battle of Santa Cruz, Guadalcanal's priceless Henderson Field remained in marine possession. That was the one fact that mattered most.

NAVAL BATTLE OF GUADALCANAL

The climax of the Guadalcanal campaign came on 13-14 November 1942. A major surface engagement in 'Ironbottom Sound' immediately north of the island was fought on the night of the 12th-13th, with the Americans losing two light cruisers and four destroyers. Japan lost a pair of destroyers, and left behind the crippled battleship *Hiei*. Unable to manoeuvre out of range, *Hiei* was subjected to a day-long series of air strikes throughout the 13th.

Three TBF squadrons operating from Henderson Field made five attacks upon the Japanese dreadnought. Fifteen sorties were flown by VT-10, six by VT-8, and ten by the first Marine TBF unit, VMSB-131. From these sorties, 26 torpedoes were launched and ten hits claimed. Battered and blazing, *Hiei* finally sank that evening, the first enemy battleship sunk by US torpedo bombers. The Avenger crews celebrated their success with mixed drinks of fruit juice and torpedo alcohol. And while Navy and Marine SBDs contributed to the sinking, the TBF squadrons could claim the major share of the aviators' credit.

Next day, 14 November, was equally frantic. In a bold daylight reinforcement effort, the Japanese sent nearly two-dozen ships – transports escorted by destroyers– down the island chain toward Guadalcanal. Search aeroplanes found a cruiser force in the same area, which was attacked by US Navy and Marine aircraft. VT-10 and VMSB-131 each contributed three Avengers to the strike, and they put four torpedoes into the 9000-ton *Kinugasa*. As the TBFs pulled off the target, the heavy cruiser was burning fiercely, on her way to the bottom.

The Japanese transports were subjected to repeated, merciless air attack. Henderson Field was to have been knocked out by heavy shelling, but the much fought-over airstrip remained operational. In the final major US torpedo action of the campaign, VT-10 skipper Lt Albert 'Scoofer' Coffin led seven VT-10 aeroplanes in a devastating attack on one column of transports. The *Enterprise* pilots scored three hits which sank two ships.

By the end of the day the Japanese effort was almost completely thwarted. Though nobody knew it at the time, the defeat of the reinforcement effort marked the final crisis which Americans would face at Guadalcanal. Another three months would pass before the island was declared secure, but the outcome was no longer uncertain.

Secretary of the Navy James Forrestal later said that Grumman saved Guadalcanal. He was thinking mainly of the F4F Wildcat, and although the statement ignored the crucial contribution of the Douglas SBD, there was some merit in the assertion. The Avenger, which had suffered so badly in its debut at Midway, more than proved itself with a contribution that far outweighed its small numbers.

MARINES

Gradually, more marine TBFs arrived in the Solomons. Three squadrons operated from the advanced beach head at Torokina Strip in early November 1943 as VMTB-143, -232 and -233 supported infantry units on Bougainville. The same squadrons were deeply involved in the reduction of the Japanese naval-air complex at Rabaul, New Britain, well into 1944.

Typical of TBF aircrew operating against Rabaul was Lester T Ludwig, a turret gunner in VMTB-242. He recalled;

'The main problem on Bougainville was the continual shelling of the airstrip at night. Just after dark they would start falling. It was thought that the Japs had some large artillery on rails that were under cover, and at night they would roll them out, drop a few shells, and move back under cover. On several occasions, planes from "242" would leave in the morning trying to locate the guns, but without success.

'The strikes over Rabaul were mainly on the airstrips. However, at times the town was hit with incendiary bombs. Our squadron would leave Bougainville with a squadron of SBDs and fighter escorts. The dive-bombers were the first in, trying to knock out the anti-aircraft guns. Then we would attack from three directions in what was called a glide bomb run, drop the bombs, and leave as quickly as possible. The glide would start from 10,000 to 15,000 ft. We would drop our bombs at about 1500 ft, then descend to the treetops and move out. This was when the turret gunner would start strafing.

'I experienced two crash landings, with no injuries. The crash landing on Bougainville was due to heavy AA fire over the town of Rabaul. The plane was shot up badly from an almost direct hit underneath. We made it back to Bougainville and my pilot, 1Lt G H Thompson, brought the plane in. I received one small piece of flak in my left shoulder, and a small calibre bullet went through my water canteen without hitting me.'

In the summer of 1944 VMTB-131 (previously redesignated a TorpRon) was joined by -242, providing close air support to marine rifle companies in the Marianas. Ludwig was still with -242, and described the transition;

'We were sent to Pearl Harbor for more training in anti-submarine patrol. After returning to the South Pacific, our new TBMs were equipped with depth charges and rockets. Our squadron was then sent to the Marianas and helped the marine ground forces by flying from the island of Tinian. We also began anti-sub patrol missions.

'In March 1945 notification came that the marines had landed on the south beach of Iwo Jima and were working north. This was the clue for us to take off. We had just enough gas to fly from Tinian to Iwo (about 800 miles), and if the airfield wasn't secured, we would have to land on an aircraft carrier lying offshore. When we approached Iwo Jima, all we could see was smoke and dust. While flying over the island I called our pilot and asked him where the airstrip was because everything looked the same – all torn up. We did manage to land between the shell holes and refuel and load up with bombs which had been brought up from the beach. We

Cpl Lester T Ludwig was a TBF gunner with VMTB-242 during 1944-45. His first combat tour was spent at Bougainville, in the upper Solomon Islands, and he subsequently flew missions in the Marianas and Bonins. In his wartime career Ludwig survived two crash landings – one on Bougainville and another on Iwo Jima (Ludwig)

flew ground support for thefront lines until the island was secured. We then started anti-sub patrols again, until our return to Tinian.

'At this time the squadron was put on notice to be ready to leave again – rumour said Formosa – but another squadron relieved us and VMTB-242 returned to the States.

'The TBF and TBM were sometimes called "flying coffins", but we aircrew felt that they were the safest plane flying. The large engine was dependable, and the large bomb bay withstood water and crash landings very well. My second crash landing was at Iwo Jima, and fortunately there were again no injuries.'

In the Central Pacific, VMTB-134 was involved in the bloody conquest of Peleliu in August 1944. Operating within 'landing gear' range of the frontlines, marine aviators joked that they hardly had time to raise their wheels before arriving over their target area.

The Okinawa campaign (Operation *Iceberg*) also involved marine TBMs. Beginning in April 1945, the Tactical Air Force on Okinawa provided not only direct support of marine and army infantry, but patrolled the surrounding ocean as well. Solomons veterans VMTB-131 and -232 were both heavily committed.

Finally, carrier-based marine Avengers also made their presence felt. VMTB-233 supported the Okinawa landings from the second *Block Island* while -143, aboard *Gilbert Islands*, likewise struck the Ryukyus before moving on to the Balikpapan operation. Two other 'leather-neck' TBM units committed to combat were VMTB-234 in *Vella Gulf* and -132 aboard *Cape Gloucester*. The latter CVEs were detailed to operations in the Central Pacific and the East China Sea, respectively. Ironically, despite the dedicated VMTB designation, apparently none of these squadrons used torpedoes in combat after the Solomons campaign.

However, such was the Marine Corps' commitment to heavy attack that six TBM training squadrons were based at MCAS El Toro and Santa Barbara, California. Additionally, no fewer than nine operational squadrons were working toward overseas deployments when the Pacific war finally ended.

The uniformity of makings indicates that this is a navy squadron of 16 or more TBFs in late 1943. The overall colour scheme is blue-grey over medium grey, a relatively unusual combination with the late-war national insignia of blue background for the cockade and bars without the interim red border. Note the solitary SBD manoeuvring to the left of the formation (*Grumman*)

Returned from one of the November 1943 strikes against Rabaul, wounded VT-12 gunner Kenneth Bratton is assisted from his turret by *Saratoga* flightdeck crewmen. The two missions, flown on 5 and 11 November, resulted in the crippling of several Japanese warships, which eased pressure on the Bougainville beach head. Eleven carrier-based TBFs were lost to all causes in these operations (*Grumman*)

CENTRAL PACIFIC

From late 1943, increasing numbers of TBF-1Cs arrived in fleet units. The Avenger's design 'stretch' and operational versatility were quickly recognised and exploited, and nowhere more so than in the nocturnal role.

During the Gilbert Islands operation of November 1943, the *Enterprise* air group commander committed his 'Black Panther' teams to combat. Lt Cdr E H 'Butch' O'Hare was already a legendary fighter pilot, but he drilled his hand-picked 'Panthers' in preparation for night intercepts of enemy aircraft. With a radar-equipped Avenger guiding two conventional F6F-3 Hellcats, the plan was to have shipboard controllers vector the team onto Japanese bombers, at which time the TBF radar operator would complete the interception.

The first test came on the night of 26 November. Teamed with Lt Cdr John C Phillips of VT-6, O'Hare and his VF-2 wingman hunted inbound Mitsubishi G4M 'Bettys' in the gathering dark. Phillips' radar operator, Lt(jg) H B Rand, put Phillips onto two 'Bettys' in succession. The fighters were poorly positioned to attack, so Phillips bored in to minimum range and downed both with his wing-mounted .50-cals.

Calling for a rendezvous, O'Hare's Hellcats joined on the Avenger as more 'Bettys' appeared. In a brief, confusing, nocturnal shoot-out, the TBF gunner and one or more 'Bettys' exchanged fire. Evidence indicates that O'Hare, between the TBF and the Japanese, was struck by machine gun fire from a 'Betty' above and behind him. His F6F glided down out of sight and he was lost forever. Phillips was killed in action shortly afterwards, but he and O'Hare had proved the concept of carrier-based nightfighters.

Meanwhile, another *Enterprise* aviator was developing the Avenger's considerable night attack potential. Lt Cdr William I Martin, formerly of VS-10, had assumed command of VT-10 during the ship's 1943 refit on the West Coast. As a junior officer, he had written the first instrument training manual for carrier aviators, and by 1944 he was recognised

A typical *Essex*-class air group prepared for a 'deck-load launch' of at least 12 F6F-3 fighters, 14 TBF-1C Avengers and 7 SB2C-1 Helldivers. The intricate flightdeck choreography essential for getting a mission airborne is evident here: chock men ready to put aircraft in motion; directors serving as 'traffic cops'; and plane handlers standing by to help swing folded wings into place (*Grumman*)

A TBF makes a run on a burning Japanese cargo ship during the strike against Kwajalein Atoll on 4 December 1943. The operation inaugurated a succession of strikes against enemy naval-air facilities in the Marshall Islands, with Avenger squadrons flying ground support missions in the month-long operation against 'Kwaj', Maloelap, and Wotje Atolls (*Grumman*)

The meaning of close air support. US Marines watch a flight of five Avengers attacking Japanese positions on the north end of Namur Island in early February 1944. Scenes like this were repeated across the Central Pacific as TBFs provided tactical air cover for American infantrymen in a variety of campaigns (*Grumman*)

as the navy's authority on the subject. Furthermore, during training at NAS Seattle, Washington, experiments with airborne radar showed that ships could be detected at 35 to 50 nautical miles, and Martin devoted much time to perfecting the night attack concept.

One of Martin's most enthusiastic pilots was Lt(jg) Charles E Henderson III, who recalled;

'Protected by a young, aggressive admiral named Arthur Radford, Bill drove us hard. Nothing but instruments and night operations. Then at Maui we did long night searches and attacks against friendly ships. As our skills developed, we improved our equipment. Bill's imagination fired us with innovation. We regrouped our instruments, developed indirect red lighting, an alarm buzzer on our radio altimeters and a night gunsight. What we couldn't requisition, we stole!'

Ironically, after months of preparation, Martin was unable to fly his squadron's first night combat mission owing to a broken elbow suffered in a ball game. However, he described VT-10's landmark success at Truk Atoll on the night of 16-17 February 1944;

'The squadron was so well trained that it really wasn't necessary for me to be there. Lt Van Eason led the mission, and used what we called our standard attack. You pick up an initial point, and the planes go in a couple of minutes apart, and then come back to a rendezvous point for return to the carrier. This gives you some mutual support and mutual navigation.

'Our 12 planes went in there, looking for Japanese shipping, and each one had four 500-lb bombs. They all made four passes, and they weren't going to waste any of them. Our normal attack was at 250 ft and about 150 knots indicated, so we could maintain a steady altitude. We had a procedure that when your target disappeared under your nose, you'd count "One alligator two", and pickle a bomb, and you'd hit the waterline of a ship almost every time. The bombs had a slight delay so they would penetrate the hull of a merchant ship and let the plane pass over before exploding.

'Anyway, our planes achieved surprise and picked their targets carefully. There was a hospital ship in there which we didn't want to hit, and we had pretty good intelligence on where it was. I believe the 12 planes got 13 Japanese ships that were sunk or beached, and we lost one TBF. I'm told the Japanese confirmed after the war that our estimate of damage inflicted was accurate. The great thing, though, was that half of our bombs were hits that night. It was more than you normally get during a daytime attack, with attendant higher losses.'

PHILIPPINE SEA

The two greatest naval battles of World War 2 were fought in the wide expanse of the Western Pacific called the Philippine Sea. They occurred four months apart, involving hundreds of warships and thousands of aircraft. Their like will never be seen again.

The First Battle of the Philippine Sea – better known in aviation circles as 'The Great Marianas Turkey Shoot'—was sparked by the American invasion of Saipan. With Guam and Tinian, Saipan was too valuable for Japan to lose if there were to be any hope of stopping the Allied advance. Therefore, the Imperial Navy came out of hiding for the first time in nearly two years. The Japanese despatched nine carriers and numerous escorts to contest the Saipan landings in June 1944. The American carrier commander, Vice Adm Marc Mitscher, had 15

Among the escort carriers involved in the early phase of the Central Pacific campaign was *Natoma Bay*, operating Composite Squadron 63. Seen over Wotje Atoll on 9 February 1944, these TBF-1Cs display the squadron's unusual markings – both a vertical stripe parallel to the rudder hinge line and an alpha-numeric designation on the fuselage (*Author's collection*)

Torpedo wakes criss-cross Truk Lagoon during the major attack by the Fast Carrier Task Force on 16-17 February. The freighter in the foreground has just been struck forward of amidships, while another 'fish' seemed headed for a hit. Some 200,000 tons of naval and merchant shipping was claimed sunk at Truk, in large part by TBFs armed with bombs as well as torpedoes (*Grumman*)

flattops embarking 900 aircraft, including 185 TBFs and TBMs. Additionally, Task Force 52 deployed eight escort carriers in two groups with a total of 83 Avengers.

Avenger Squadrons of Task Force 58, 13 June 1944

VT-1	USS *Yorktown* (CV 10)	17 TBF/TBM-1C
VT-2	USS *Hornet* (CV 12)	18 TBF/TBM-1C
VT-8	USS *Bunker Hill* (CV 17)	18 TBF/TBM-1C
VT-10	USS *Enterprise* (CV 10)	14 TBF/TBM-1C
VT-14	USS *Wasp* (CV 18)	18 TBF/TBM-1C/D
VT-15	USS *Essex* (CV 9)	20 TBF/TBM-1C
VT-16	USS *Lexington* (CV 16)	18 TBF/TBM-1C
VT-24	USS *Belleau Wood* (CVL 24)	9 TBF/TBM-1C
VT-25	USS *Cowpens* (CVL 25)	9 TBF/TBM-1C
VT-27	USS *Princeton* (CVL 23)	9 TBM-1C
VT-28	USS *Monterey* (CVL 26)	8 TBM-1C
VT-31	USS *Cabot* (CVL 28)	9 TBF/TBM-1C
VT-50	USS *Bataan* (CVL 29)	9 TBF/TBM-1C
VT-51	USS *San Jacinto* (CVL 30)	9 TBM-1C

Avenger Squadrons of Task Group 52, 13 June 1944

VC-3	USS *Kalinin Bay* (CVE 68)	9 TBM-1C
VC-4	USS *White Plains* (CVE 66)	12 TBF/TBM-1C
VC-5	USS *Kitkun Bay* (CVE 71)	8 TBM-1C
VC-10	USS *Gambier Bay* (CVE 73)	9 TBM-1C
VC-33	USS *Coral Sea* (CVE 57)	12 TBF/TBM-1C
VC-41	USS *Corregidor* (CVE 58)	12 TBM-1C
VC-65	USS *Midway* (CVE 63)	9 TBM-1C
VC-68	USS *Fanshaw Bay* (CVE 70)	12 TBM-1C

Note: CVE 57 was subsequently renamed *Anzio* and CVE 63 *St Lo*. Composite squadrons also operated 12 to 16 FM-2 Wildcats.

BATTLE FOR THE MARIANAS

Avengers of Mitscher's Task Force 58 and the escort carrier groups spent the first few days of the campaign in routine chores: bombing, ground support, anti-submarine patrol and reconnaissance. In the great air battle of 19 June, 15 Hellcat units destroyed the Japanese air groups as they struck four times at the fast carrier force. Not until the 20th did TBFs play a larger role in the battle, and then it was crucial.

Two Japanese carriers had been sunk by US submarines on the 19th, but the remaining seven fled westward after losing the majority of their aircraft. All through the morning and afternoon of the 20th, TBFs and F6Fs searched for the retreating enemy without success. It appeared that the quarry would escape without being brought to battle.

Then, at 1450, two Air Group 10 search teams made contact far to the westward. Each team consisted of two Avengers and a Hellcat, the teams being led by Lt Robert S Nelson and Lt(jg) Robert R Jones. Nelson first noticed a ripple on the horizon slightly to port of his flight path. Rain squalls obscured visibility, but Lt(jg) Ed Laster of Jones' team, also flying a TBF, sighted the enemy fleet a few minutes later from the adjoining sector. The two *Enterprise* teams had approached the fleet from opposite directions! Nelson and Jones transmitted Vice Adm Ozawa's position and composition to Mitscher within minutes.

As Nelson stayed in the area amplifying the contact and updating his reports, Jones scouted for TF-58, repeating the message. He recalled;

'My most vivid recollections of the search flight are the Japanese carrier leaving a circular wake as it turned after we had been in view of it for four or five minutes while we circled, double-checking the plot of our position. As we were returning after transmitting the contact report, I also recall the sight of fighter pilot Ned Colgan's F6F as it swooped down and away in pursuit of the Japanese plane we spotted heading on an opposite course, possibly carrying a contact report of its own. The splash of the Jap plane, shot down by Colgan in the distance, was in a way anti-climactic.

'The sight of the outgoing TBFs and other attack planes passing on opposite course high overhead was most impressive, and the most clearly remembered event of the day.'

It was indeed impressive, as some 230 aeroplanes had been launched from TF-58 upon receipt of the Avengers' reports. Among the strike group were 54 Avengers from 10 carriers. Excluding aborts, *Yorktown* and *Bunker Hill* both launched eight aircraft. Seven took off from Wasp, six from *Lexington* and five from *Enterprise*. Three light carriers – *Belleau Wood*, *Monterey* and *Cabot* – each put up four. Finally, *San Jacinto's* VT-51 launched two 'torpeckers'. However, fewer than 20 Avengers were armed with torpedoes. The rest carried 500-lb bombs.

Five Avengers aborted the mission with mechanical problems: two each from VT-1 and 2, and one from VT-16. That left 54 TBFs/TBMs to attack the Japanese fleet just as the red sun was setting over the western horizon of the Philippine Sea.

The Japanese had known they would be attacked, and put up as strong a CAP as possible – about 75 aeroplanes. Most were A6M5 Zero fighters, but the defenders also included some dive-bombers.

Despite the great disparity of numbers, the Japanese pilots proved generally aggressive. VT-2 off *Hornet* was the only TBF unit that was not engaged by enemy aircraft, the other TorpRons reporting attacks by 43 'bandits', but the escorting Hellcats took good care of the strike aeroplanes. Only two TBF squadrons were molested seriously enough to fire in self-defence. *Enterprise's* VT-10 saw 12 hostiles, and two gunners fired at those which came close enough. One Zero fell into the water, but *Lexington's* VT-16 was not so fortunate. Attacked from above and behind by 11 fighters, the score was even at one Zero and one Avenger shot down.

The unfortunate *Lexington* flier was Lt(jg) Warren E McLellan, the only TBF pilot shot down by an enemy aircraft over the Japanese fleet. But his luck was not all bad.

Lt Robert R 'Railroad' Jones deplanes after recovering safely back aboard *Enterprise* at the end of a rough mission over Truk on 16 February 1944. As Jones exits the cockpit with his cardboard, VT-10 crewmen survey the flak damage to his TBF-1C, which shows both entrance and exit holes in the leading edge of the port wing (*Author's collection*)

The material price of victory was not only measured in ships sunk and aircraft downed. TBF-1C BuNo 24412 rests on the beach at Gnome, New Caledonia, in December 1943, having been stripped of most of its useable equipment: outer wing panels, 'tail feathers', access hatches, armament and some instruments (*Author's collection*)

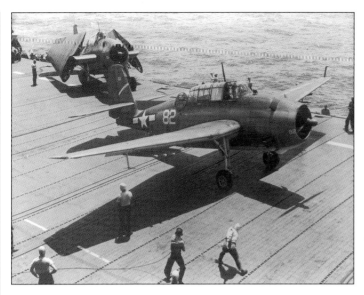

With cowl flaps open for cooling and wing flaps partly lowered for maximum lift, 'Coal 82' gets the 'Go' signal from *Yorktown's* launch officer during Operation *Forager*, in the Marianas, in June 1944 (*Author's collection*)

Ens F T Long of Torpedo Squadron Two wrote off TBM-1C BuNo 45593 in a crash-landing aboard *Hornet* on 19 June. Number 93 had already sustained previous damage, attested by the still unpainted fabric patch on the rudder (*Author's collection*)

McLellan and both his crewmen survived 22 hours in the water before being rescued. Upon his return he reported;

'I heard various people say over the radio that Zekes were in the air, and soon afterwards about 50 tracers appeared to pass through my plane and go directly out ahead and slightly upward, as though an enemy fighter was making a run from below and astern. The horizontal stabiliser of the TBF apparently hid the Zeke from the view of my turret gunner because he had been alerted to the presence of fighters ahead and had not been keeping a careful lookout (astern).

'As soon as the first bullets passed through the plane, I pulled back quickly on the stick to avoid other possible bursts, but a fire started in the cockpit on the port side. The cockpit was ablaze before I could find the microphone. However, the crewmen fortunately realised the gravity of our situation and were ready to parachute almost as soon as I. Leaning out of the cockpit as far as possible, I placed my feet upon the instrument panel and pushed myself out.

'Before pulling my ripcord I waited until I had fallen clear of the area where most of the Japanese planes were, and where the heavy anti-aircraft shells were bursting. When the parachute opened, I seemed to be suspended in mid-air, where I was in an excellent position to observe the battle going on around and below me. The attack on a *Shokaku* class carrier was only about half completed at this time, but I had seen two good bomb hits on her before being attacked by the Zeke, so she must have received considerable damage. However, my attention soon became occupied with trying to see where the bullets were coming from that were passing nearby. Shrapnel was falling in the water all around, and I saw a Zeke strafe an object in the water, which may have been our TBF, almost directly underneath me.

'So much had been happening that I failed to prepare for a water landing until I saw the water coming up to meet me. By working fast, however, I removed most of the parachute harness before hitting the water. Since the buoyancy of my backpack tended to hold me face down in the water, I had to cut one side of the strap. However, I was unable to locate the buckle that fastened the one-man liferaft

to the parachute, and as the 'chute was becoming water-soaked and was almost pulling me under, I was afraid to fasten the raft to my life jacket. My knife was lost in trying to cut the raft from the parachute, and soon the raft was gone, too. The backpack was the only thing saved, and it became water-soaked after about eight hours and had to be abandoned.'

The next morning, search aircraft dropped liferafts to McLellan and his crew, and later that day they were rescued and returned to CV 16.

The Zeke downed by McLellan's unit was credited to the turret gunner in the CO's aircraft. AMM1/c J W Webb, flying with Lt Norman A Sterrie, saw the Zeke make a level run from the 5:30 position as VT-16 withdrew after its attack. Webb could not depress his .50-cal enough to fire during the Zeke's run, but neither did the Japanese score any hits. As the fighter pulled away, it climbed slightly and Webb fired about 20 rounds into its underside. The Mitsubishi began to burn, went into the water at a 45-degree angle, and exploded.

While only one Avenger was lost to enemy aircraft, three fell to the heavy, multi-coloured flak. Two of *Yorktown's* VT-1 TBFs were shot down, and VT-24 from *Belleau Wood* also sustained a loss to AA fire. But the VT-24 crews obtained the best results.

Air Group 24 launched 12 aeroplanes: eight Hellcats and four Avengers. Leading the TBF division was Lt(jg) George P Brown, with Lt(jg)s Warren R Omark, Benjamin C Tate and W D Luton. All four TBF-1Cs were armed with torpedoes.

Warren Omark relates the events of that evening;

'Just prior to launching, George Brown made the statement to our skipper that we would get a carrier. I believe the distance was about 300 miles, and it gave us plenty of time to reflect and think about the forthcoming attack.

'The strike group commander led us to the Japanese fleet, and my recollection is that we were at 12,000 ft. The enemy fleet was a

On the evening of 20 June, Task Force 58 launched more than 200 aircraft on a maximum range strike against the Japanese carriers withdrawing from 'The Marianas Turkey Shoot'. *Hornet's* VT-2 contributed six Avengers to the 'Mission Beyond Darkness', flying through heavy clouds near the Japanese Mobile Fleet (*Author's collection*)

Two Japanese carriers had been sunk by US submarines on 19 June, but no American aircraft had attacked enemy 'flattops' since the Santa Cruz engagement of October 1942. Here, approaching sunset on the 20th, the heavy carrier *Zuikaku* (centre) is seen afire while still under attack. She survived damage inflicted by TBFs and SB2Cs, but succumbed to the same combination at Leyte Gulf four months later (*Grumman*)

large task force consisting of carriers, battleships, cruisers and destroyers. The light conditions were still very good at the time, and each squadron from the respective carriers selected the targets that they wanted to attack.

'"Brownie" had spotted the largest carrier, which of course was well protected by a surrounding screen. F6Fs from the *Belleau Wood* were quickly engaged in fighting off attacking Japanese airplanes, so we made the attack on the carrier with no cover. "Brownie" led us into a sharp dive at the Japanese fleet. In so doing, Luton was separated from the division and actually proceeded in an attack on another part of the fleet.'

Although it would not be known for many hours, Luton sighted a light carrier and went after it. He saw his torpedo make a normal water entry and noticed the wake heading toward the target. But in taking evasive action, Luton made a sharp 180-degree turn and could not observe the result of his attack. Apparently he missed, as no other Japanese carriers were torpedoed. Flak damage prevented Luton's bomb bay doors from closing, and the additional drag increased his fuel consumption. Flying back toward the task force, he ran out of fuel and had to ditch. Luton and his crew were rescued the next day.

Omark recalls how the attack developed against the main target;

'"Brownie", Ben Tate and I fanned out to approach from different angles. The attack course took us over the outlying screen of destroyers, then cruisers and finally the battleships. This screen had to be penetrated in order to reach the proper range for launching torpedoes against the carrier. The AA fire was very intense and I took as much evasive action as I could to avoid being hit.

'During the attack, "Brownie's" aircraft was hit (by flak) and caught fire. I think one of the remarkable stories of the war then took place. George Platz and Ellis Babcock were the two crewmen in "Brownie's" plane, and on knowing their plane was afire, and unable to reach "Brownie" on the intercom, they parachuted and actually witnessed the attack from the water. They remained there all night and were found and rescued the next day by search planes.

'We came in about 400 ft off the water to get a satisfactory launch of our torpedoes and dropped them on converging courses which

The only carrier sunk during the famous 'Mission Beyond Darkness' was *Hiyo*, which was one of the newest warships in the Imperial Navy. These four VT-24 crews were responsible for its demise, having attacked the Mobile Fleet with torpedo-armed Avengers on 20 June. The three surviving pilots (standing) are, left to right: Lt(jg)s W R Omark, B C Tate and Ens W D Luton. The division leader, lost on the mission, was Lt(jg) G P Brown (inset). Aircrewmen are J E Prince, R E Ranes, J Dobbs, G Platz, P Whiting, J A Brookbank and E E Babcock. Not pictured was J F Siwicki (*B C Tate*)

Lt(jg) George P Brown (centre) with his crew, ARM2/c Ellis C Babcock (right) and AMM2/c George H Platz (left) on *Belleau Wood's* flightdeck. With his Avenger set afire from flak hits, Brown ordered Babcock and Platz to bail out, then pressed home his attack against *Hiyo*, which the two aircrewmen saw capsize that night. They were rescued to confirm the carrier's destruction, but Brown did not return (*B C Tate*)

presumably did not allow the carrier to take effective evasive action. Platz and Babcock later reported that we did hit the carrier and that it later sank. It was reported as a *Hayataka* class CV, but later we understood this was a *Hiyo* class ship.'

The latter information was correct. There was in fact no *Hayataka* class in the Imperial Navy – probably a translation error by US intelligence. The VT-24 had attacked *Hiyo* herself, lead ship of the class which displaced over 24,000 tons and measured some 720 ft overall.

Lt(jg) Ben Tate also had a harrowing experience during the attack;

'George Brown was an aggressive aviator. He came in on the ship ahead, and to the port side, just seconds ahead of me on the starboard side. I saw Brown's "fish" hit the water close in and in perfect position. He dropped on the port side but the carrier was turning through his "fish", and it would have hit the starboard side. Brown pulled out to port and I lost sight of him flying down the run mounts on that side.

'At one point I found myself going at 340 knots, which is near or past the red line. I wanted to drop at 200 ft and 200 knots, which I did, by pulling the throttle all the way back. I remember feeling rather stupid hearing my wheel warning horn blowing as I flew through the Jap fleet. We had everybody shooting at us.

'As I flew down the side of the carrier I thought I saw tracers in the cockpit. I decided this was delusion until one hit my hand, taking off a few inches of the top of the stick. I retired close to a battleship which fired broadsides into the water in front of me, but when I got to the splashes, there was no effect. I do remember that when the battleship fired its broadside the whole side of the ship looked red.'

Like Omark, Tate was pursued by Zeros, but evaded them in cloud. Heading toward the rendezvous point, he came upon Brown, flying erratically into the gathering darkness. Tate attempted to keep Brown in sight but finally lost track of him and proceeded alone. When the battle-damaged TBF ran out of fuel short of the task force, Tate made a successful water landing. He was the rescued next day with his crew.

Meanwhile, Warren Omark had joined on Brown's fire-blackened TBF and briefly flew formation, hoping to lead him to safety. However, Brown was obviously wounded and, unable to maintain course, drifted off into the dark. Omark dead-reckoned back to TF-58, recovering aboard *Lexington* after more than five hours in the air;

'We remained overnight and were launched next day to return to *Belleau Wood*. There we learned that Ben Tate and Luton were safe and that Platz and Babcock had been rescued, but that "Brownie" was missing. It was then reported that we had sunk the Japanese carrier.'

Hiyo was the only carrier lost to the 200-aircraft strike. Others were damaged by TBFs, SBDs and SB2Cs carrying bombs, but the VT-24 trio with its torpedoes claimed the sole success against a combatant vessel. A pair of oilers was sunk by *Wasp's* Air Group 14, but otherwise the Imperial Navy escaped from the Marianas without further loss.

In exchange, nearly half of the 227 American aircraft on the mission were lost. Only about 20 were attributed to enemy action – the majority splashed down out of fuel, or were wrecked in landing accidents. The TBF and TBM casualties were typical: four shot down over the Japanese fleet and 25 lost to operational causes. This amounted to 53

Lt R P Gift enjoys a cigarette and some liquid refreshment in the light carrier *Monterey's* ready room after the hectic dusk attack. Gift was one of 54 Avenger pilots that participated in the mission, with its objective still chalked on VT-28's blackboard behind him (*Grumman*)

per cent of the Avengers that made the attack. But efficient rescue work kept human losses to fewer than 50 pilots and aircrewmen. It could have been much worse.

Avengers Launched on 20 June 1944*
(*excludes four aborts)

Task Group 58.1

Yorktown (CV 10)	VT-1	8	Lost 5
Hornet (CV 12)	VT-2	6	Lost 2
Belleau Wood (CVL 24	VT-24	4	Lost 3?
Bataan (CVL 29)	VT-50	0	

Task Group 58.2

Bunker Hill (CV 17)	VT-8	8	Lost 5
Wasp (CV 18)	VT-14	7	Lost 3
Cabot (CVL 28)	VT-31	4	Lost 2
Monterey (CVL 26)	VT-28	4	Lost 1

Task Group 58.3

Lexington (CV 16)	VT-16	6	Lost 3
Enterprise (CV 6)	VT-10	5	Lost 4
San Jacinto (CVL 30)	VT-51	2	Lost 1
Princeton (CVL 23)	VT-27	0	

Task Group 58.4

Essex (CV 9)	VT-15	0	
Cowpens (CVL 25)	VT-25	0	
Langley (CVL 27)	VT-32	0	

Of the 29 losses, three were pushed overboard from *Enterprise*, *Cabot* and *Hornet*. Heaviest personnel losses on the mission were sustained by Torpedo One, which lost six men in combat. Four other fliers were lost operationally, including a VT-8 crew last seen in the area of TF-58.

However, Fifth Fleet's rescue operation proved spectacularly successful. At least 67 Avenger pilots or aircrewmen were saved from the ocean, including 56 by destroyers and six by cruisers. OS2U Kingfisher

The Marianas campaign continued well after the climactic Battle of the Philippine Sea in late June. This VC-11 aircraft, operating off the escort carrier *Nehenta Bay*, patrols over Tinian on 25 July (*Author's collection*)

floatplanes from the cruisers *Boston* and *Canberra* rescued five more TBM airmen.

In all, 37 TBFs or TBMs were lost to various causes on 20 June, including five from the escort carriers. It was the largest one-day attrition thus far, but worse lay ahead.

INTERIM ACTIONS

Following the Philippine Sea battle, conquest of the Marianas was a foregone conclusion, and the fast carriers continued their westward march. With the Philippines as the next major objective, preparatory strikes were conducted in the Bonins and Palaus, which were positioned to threaten American naval operations in the Western Pacific prior to Leyte Gulf.

'Any landing you can swim away from!' BuNo 46203 went over the side of *Marcus Island* on 8 August 1944, but Lt(jg) A M Peyou and his VC-21 crew appear to be in no danger as the TBM-1C floats despite the loss of much of its port wing (*Author's collection*)

Of special concern was the Bonin group, a cluster of volcanic islands some 750 miles south of Tokyo. The largest and most significant was Iwo Jima, with three airfields. However, seaborne communications were also targeted, and in August 1944 the fast carriers set their sights on Japanese shipping in the area. The event marked the debut of new torpedoes for the Avenger squadrons, including *Franklin's* VT-13, led by Lt Cdr Larry French, who recalled;

'The first use of ring-tail torpedoes was on 4 August 1944 against a Japanese convoy of six transports, with nine destroyer types escorting. Before launch, our admiral told me, "I do not want to include in my action report some shipping damaged . . . I want them sunk!"

'Air Group 13 attacked this convoy about 70 miles west of Iwo Jima. Our strike included 12 Hellcat fighters to strafe and suppress AA fire, 30 SB2C dive-bombers and my 16 TBMs. The bombers attacked first and scored no direct hits. As the last VB pulled away, the guns ceased firing and all seemed quiet. Then suddenly it happened. I couldn't believe it! The convoy made a 45-degree port turn toward us. I immediately ordered, "Attack, attack, attack". Before launch I had briefed the squadron that each four-plane division would concentrate on one ship for sure kills. However, due to the sudden attack situation, some pilots in the last division veered off and took shots at the two other ships.

'We dived down over the left side of the screen and broke through the AA fire. We were inside the screen, approaching the torpedo release point at 220-240 knots at 400 ft. Of course, the convoy opened fire with everything it had, but it was too late. We all came through the AA fire, and had great torpedo shots at the transports at very short range.

'VT-13 claimed the sinking of all six transports. This was confirmed by the air group commander, and later by surface ships sent to investigate the area. It is my firm belief that had VT-13 used the regular aerial torpedo, dropping at 100-110 knots at 100 ft, we could not have successfully made this attack, as our losses would have been excessive. But we lost no planes or crews, and had heavy damage to one TBM and light damage to three others. From then on we used the ring-tails in the Sibuyan Sea and other Philippine areas.'

LEYTE GULF

The Second Battle of the Philippine Sea, like the first, was better known by another name. More frequently this epic naval-air clash has been called the Battle of Leyte Gulf, for it was conducted as a result of Gen Douglas MacArthur's promised return to the Philippines. It was also the last major fleet engagement ever fought, lasting three days.

With General Motors production increasing monthly, 27 of the 34 CV and CVE torpedo and composite squadrons were equipped wholly with TBMs.

Avenger Squadrons of Task Force 38, October 1944

VT-7	USS *Hancock* (CV 19)	18 TBM-1C
VT-11	USS *Hornet* (CV 12)	18 TBF/TBM-1C
VT-13	USS *Franklin* (CV 13)	18 TBM-1C
VT-14	USS *Wasp* (CV 18)	18 TBF/TBM-1C/D
VT-15	USS *Essex* (CV 9)	20 TBF/TBM-1C
VT-18	USS *Intrepid* (CV 11)	18 TBM-1C
VT-19	USS *Lexington* (CV 16)	18 TBM-1C
VT-20	USS *Enterprise* (CV 6)	19 TBM-1C
VT-21	USS *Belleau Wood* (CVL 24)	9 TBM-1C
VT-22	USS *Cowpens* (CVL 25)	9 TBM-1C
VT-27	USS *Princeton* (CVL 23)	9 TBM-1C
VT-28	USS *Monterey* (CVL 26)	9 TBM-1C
VT-29	USS *Cabot* (CVL 28)	9 TBF/TBM-1C
VT(N)-41	USS *Independence* (CVL 22)	8 TBM-1D
VT-44	USS *Langley* (CVL 27)	9 TBM-1C
VT-51	USS *San Jacinto* (CVL 30)	7 TBM-1C

TORPEDO PLANES AGAINST BATTLESHIPS

Perhaps the single largest aerial torpedo action of the war occurred in the Sibuyan Sea on 24 October 1944. Japanese Vice Adm Kurita's powerful surface force of five battleships, 13 cruisers and 15 destroyers was headed for San Bernardino Strait to contest the amphibious landings on the east coast of Leyte. US submarines sank two cruisers on the 23rd, but still the armada continued east. The skipper of *Franklin's* torpedo squadron, Lt Cdr Larry French, describes what happened;

'On 23 October, reports started to filter in of Japanese fleet units on the move toward the Philippines. On the 24th two large

Among the new carriers joining the fleet in the summer of 1944 was *Franklin*, embarking Air Group 13. These nine VT-13 pilots sank six Japanese transports near the Bonin Islands on 4 August in the first combat use of the 'ringtail' aerial torpedo. The squadron commander, Lt Cdr Larry French, had worked hard to gain approval for the modified weapon before embarking for the Western Pacific (*Author's collection*)

Torpedo Two's well-travelled No 95 chalked up an impressive record during the Hornet deployment. The plane captain sits in his TBF-1C while a photographer records the Avenger's statistics: 53 bombs and three torpedoes, representing strike missions flown between March and September 1944. In that time the squadron struck targets in the Palaus, Carolines, the Bonins, New Guinea, the Marianas and, finally, the Philippines (*Author's collection*)

groups of heavy warships were spotted closing on Leyte from different directions. We waited anxiously all that morning for further information on their positions. Finally, about 1500 word came, "Pilots man your planes. Target: Japanese fleet in the Sibuyan Sea".

'There were other US carrier groups in the area, but we were not co-ordinated. Our attack was to be a combined bombing-torpedo

Carrying HVAR aerial rockets, a division of TBF- and TBM-1C Avengers from VT-15, off the *Essex*, is seen en route to its target. Torpedo Fifteen broke into combat in May 1944, and contributed to the air group's record total of enemy tonnage sunk before completing its deployment in November. The relieving squadron, VT-4, took over these same aircraft and continued flying with the same markings (*Author's collection*)

attack, and the *Franklin* strike contained 24 dive-bombers, about 12 fighter escorts and 10 TBMs with ring-tail torpedoes. The group proceeded on a west-northwest course at 17,000 ft across Samar Island to the Sibuyan Sea – a distance of 250 miles. No enemy fighters were sighted and visibility at the target was good.

'On arriving at the scene, I observed that two groups of Japanese ships were already employing their air defence tactics and steaming in circles. This would present some problems for a torpedo attack against these heavy fleet units. We would attack two target groups simultaneously, hoping to get a shot off the bow of a heavy ship as it was coming around. Our formation approached from the east, with half the bombers and torpedo planes going for battleships to the south, and half towards heavy ships to the north.'

Part of the reason the Japanese armada was scattered was that the giant battleship *Musashi* had been previously damaged and was lagging behind her sister *Yamato*. But both super dreadnoughts retained heavy defensive screens composed of cruisers and destroyers, not to mention three lesser battleship. French continues;

'The SB2Cs moved over the targets at 18,000 ft and commenced dive-bombing. The torpedo planes came straight in from the side, right at the circling ships, descending from 4000 ft and arriving at the release point as the last bombs were striking. During the high-speed approach the AA fire was very heavy. The battleships were even firing their main batteries at us – not directly at the planes, but to lay down a salvo in the water in front of us. The shell splashes would send up a high column of water, with the enemy hoping a plane would fly into it. I learned these tactics back in VT-5 on the old *Yorktown* before the war. Thus, I wasn't surprised, but it sure popped your "Mk 8 eyeballs"!

'These salvos were ineffective against the torpedo attack, as we were approaching the release point at about 260 knots and 600-800 ft. Our objective was to shoot across the ship's bow as it came around toward us. We did get in and all fired, but it was almost impossible to be at the proper range as the ship came by.

'My first and second divisions claimed four possible hits. Two were on the biggest battleship, the *Musashi*, one was on a cruiser, and the possible additional hit I did not see. The third and fourth divisions got a hit on a cruiser of the northern group. We lost two TBMs shot down by the thick AA fire and had one Avenger return with heavy damage.'

In all, six US air groups struck the Kurita force during the day. Some pilots flew two missions as *Intrepid*, *Cabot*, *Lexington*, *Essex*, *Franklin* and *Enterprise* flung successive strikes at the armada. It was a long, dangerous, tiring business, but it accomplished results.

Musashi, (at 64,000 tons, one of the two largest battleships ever built) succumbed to 19 torpedoes and sank in the Sibuyan Sea the evening of the 24th, whilst the heavy cruiser *Myoko* was so damaged by bombs and torpedoes that she turned back. It was carrier airpower's first great victory over battleships manoeuvring in open water. And it would not be the last.

During these strikes against Kurita's Main Force, a total of 11 TBF/TBMs were lost, including one jettisoned from *Essex*. Only four pilots and 11 aircrew were killed from these Avenger, however. Squadron aircraft losses were from VT-13 (two), VT-15 (three), VT-18 (three), VT-19 (one) and VT-29 (two). Another 11 Avengers were stricken from the Pacific Fleet strength in related operations, nine of which belonged to VT-27 when light carrier *Princeton* was sunk by a conventional dive-bombing attack.

After an all-day pummelling, Kurita was expected to abandon his mission. In fact, scout aeroplanes informed Third Fleet commander William F Halsey that the Sibuyan Sea force was last seen retiring westward. But not for long. Determined to follow orders, the Japanese admiral reversed course and, unknown to his foes, resumed his journey toward San Bernardino Strait – Kurita passed through the narrow passage that night with four battleships, eight cruisers and 11 destroyers.

On the night of 24-25 October, *Independence's* dedicated night attack squadron, VT(N)-41, proved the worth of radar-equipped Avengers. Lt W R Taylor's aircrews were happy to end eight weeks of dull anti-submarine patrols with almost no night flying. Three VT(N)-41 TBM-3Ds scouted San Bernardino Strait between Leyte and Samar, taking advantage of the darkened, stormy sky. Ens Jack Dewis dropped within a few hundred feet of Vice Adm Takeo Kurita's surface force, even identifying some of the battleships by name. The alarming news that Japanese battleships and cruisers were steaming toward Leyte Gulf was passed to Adm W F Halsey's Third Fleet staff, but for reasons that still remain unclear, the report was never actually acted upon.

AMBUSH OFF SAMAR

Supporting the army landings on Leyte was the Seventh Fleet, responsible for delivering Gen

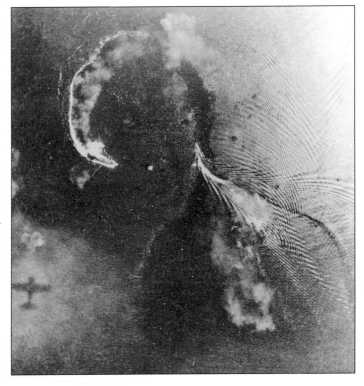

In one of naval aviation's greatest challenges, Task Force 38 air groups pounded the Japanese centre force in the Sibuyan Sea on 24 October 1944. Composed of the 'super' battleships *Musashi* and *Yamato*, the enemy surface group was attacked during a series of day-long strikes that left *Musashi* sinking. This strike photo – with the distinctive Grumman silhouette on a cloud – shows the battleship and a destroyer manoeuvring to avoid the attack (*Author's collection*)

Flightdeck crewmen from the *Independence* help fold the wings of '22 Cupid', a TBM-1D of Night Torpedo Squadron 41, in October 1944. As half of the navy's first dedicated night air group, VT(N)-41 became the pioneer among full-time nocturnal attack squadrons. Initially limited mostly to daylight operations, the squadron and air group proved the value of round the clock carrier capability, especially in tracking Vice Adm Kurita's powerful surface force through the narrow waters of the San Bernardino Strait on the night of 24-25 October (*Author's collection*)

MacArthur's troops and supplies as well as supporting them once ashore. Most of the latter duty fell to the 18 escort carriers of Task Group 77.4 under Rear Adm Thomas L Sprague. The group's three task units embarked 187 Avengers and 292 fighters, a mixture of FM-2 Wildcats and F6F Hellcats. Four of the 'jeep carriers' operated CVE air groups organised along the lines of CVL group, with one fighter and one bomber squadron. The composite squadrons, of course, flew FM-2s and TBM-3s simultaneously.

'Taffy One' (Task Unit 77.4.1)

Chenango (CVE 28)	VT-35	9 TBF-1C
Sangamon (CVE 26)	VT-37	9 TBM-1C
Suwannee (CVE 27)	VT-60	9 TBM-1C
Santee (CVE 29)	VT-26	9 TBF/TBM-1C
Petrof Bay (CVE 80)	VC-76	12 TBM-1C
Saginaw Bay (CVE 82)	VC-78	12 TBM-1C

'Taffy Two' (Task Unit 77.4.2)

Manila Bay (CVE 61)	VC-80	12 TBM-1C
Natoma Bay (CVE 62)	VC-81	12 TBM-1C
Kadashan Bay (CVE 76)	VC-20	11 TBM-1C
Marcus Island (CVE 77)	VC-21	12 TBM-1C
Savo Island (CVE 78)	VC-27	12 TBM-1C
Ommaney Bay (CVE 79)	VC-75	11 TBM-1C

'Taffy Three' (Task Unit 77.4.3)

St Lo (CVE 63)	VC-65	12 TBM-1C
White Plains (CVE 66)	VC-4	12 TBM-1C
Kalinin Bay (CVE 68)	VC-3	12 TBM/TBF-1C
Fanshaw Bay (CVE 70)	VC-68	12 TBM-1C
Kitkun Bay (CVE 71)	VC-5	12 TBM-1C
Gambier Bay (CVE 73)	VC-10	12 TBM-1C

When Kurita's powerful force emerged from the strait early on the morning of the 25th, the Japanese expected easy prey among the amphibious craft of the Leyte invasion fleet. But as Kurita steamed south toward Leyte, he encountered an escort carrier group off the east coast of Samar. This was 'Taffy Three', Task Unit 77.4.3 with six 'baby flattops' of Carrier Divisions' 25 and 26 under Rear Adm Clifton Sprague. The screen consisted of half a dozen destroyer escorts.

'Taffy Three' was in no position to fight so formidable a surface force. The escort carriers were never intended for a fleet engagement. They were equipped and trained for tactical air support of ground troops, and to provide anti-submarine protection. Hence, the six CVEs' 70-odd Avengers were armed mainly with bombs and depth charges – the 90-plus Wildcats had little more than their four .50-cal. machine guns.

Ens Hans Jensen, a TBM pilot on 'anti-sub' patrol north of 'Taffy Three', flashed the first warning shortly before 0700. He radioed Clifton Sprague and informed him that the distinctive 'pagoda' masts of Japanese battleships were visible. Radar soon confirmed the sighting.

Sprague was caught in a most unenviable situation. He could not hope to outdistance his faster opponents, and he certainly could not out-shoot them. The largest guns in his force were 5.38 'inchers' – a poor match for Kurita's battleships and cruisers, mounting everything from 6- to 18-in guns. So Sprague did the only thing he could do. He headed south toward distant help of other escort groups, ordered his ships to lay a smokescreen, and began launching aircraft. Many were unarmed.

One of the Avenger pilots who played a prominent role in this uneven battle was Lt Cdr Edward J Huxtable. As commanding officer of Composite Squadron 10 aboard *Gambier Bay*, he had a bird's eye view of the proceedings.

'I got in my plane and asked the plane captain if I had a bomb load. He said no, so I told him to call Lt Cdr Buzz Borries, the air officer, if I had time to get a load. We had not turned up the engines as yet, and I couldn't see any use going off without some ordnance. I saw Borries move forward and speak to Capt Walter Viewig, who made a sweeping motion with his arm as if he were saying, "Get 'em off!"

'About this time I was startled by what seemed a rifle shot next to my left ear. I looked and saw that it was a salvo of heavy calibre stuff splashing alongside *White Plains*. Until this moment I had no idea the enemy was so near. Now I was more than ready to get on that catapult. We turned up engines and three TBMs launched ahead of me. As I shot off, the lead plane had started his 180-degree turn for a regular carrier join-up. The ceiling was low at about 1200 ft. After I took the lead I called Adm Sprague's code name, "Bendix", and asked what our orders were. They came back in an excited voice, "Attack immediately".

'We were headed aft in relation to the ship, and with the visibility being poor, I could just see the destroyer plane guards, and shortly broke out into better visibility and higher ceilings, where I spotted four cruisers near and what appeared to be four battleships farther back in the gloom. At this moment the cruisers' bearing from our force would be off the port quarter, and our force was on an easterly course. There was no possibility of making a high-altitude attack, so I turned back over the destroyers and our carriers, and turned on a course I figured would bring us out over the Jap cruisers. I pulled up into the ceiling and started for the cruisers. What loads the other planes had I did not know, but at least we would give the Japs a scare.'

Huxtable co-ordinated both 'hot' and 'dry' attacks on the Japanese warships with his Annapolis classmate, Lt Cdr Richard Fowler of *Kitkun Bay's* VC-5. Between them, they kept an unrelenting string of CVE aircraft overhead Kurita's force, giving the impression of far greater resources than were available.

Day Two of the Battle of Leyte Gulf occurred on 25 October 1944, and saw sustained carrier strikes flown against Vice Adm Ozawa's decoy force off the north-east coast of Luzon. The flak-damaged wingtip of an Avenger attests to the accuracy of enemy AA fire as an *Ise*-class battleship and a destroyer turn in formation during a torpedo attack (*National Archives*)

Another TBM pilot overhead 'Taffy Three' was Lt(jg) Norman Johnson of *Fanshaw Bay's* VC-68. His experiences were similar to Huxtable's, with one important difference. Johnson's Avenger had four 500-lb bombs;

'Climbing at full throttle, I penetrated the lower cloud cover and levelled off at 11,000 ft. There, I took a final look at the enemy force, which was firing at our ships. The latter were steaming at full speed, trying to get sea room away from the confinement of Samar Island.

'About five miles away, I nosed down to pick up speed. The Japanese battle force at that moment was occupied in anti-aircraft protection against an air attack. Varied coloured bursts mushroomed at several levels. It was quite dense, and something I had to penetrate. Bomb bay doors remained closed as speed increased. By that time, three large battleships had entered a circle with rudders hard over and guns spitting flame. At 7000 ft I pushed over into my attack, selecting the lead battleship for my target. The interphone from my radioman reminded, "Open bomb bay doors!" I pushed the lever and the doors opened. The immediate drag was apparent as the aircraft was barrelling along by now. Bombs were armed.

'Intent on adjusting the target properly in my sight, the plane corkscrewed and suddenly the right side of the canopy peeled off. I pressed the bomb release button at what seemed the best altitude and concentrated all effort on pulling out of the dive. It was a close call as the aircraft recovered about 50 to 100 ft above the water. The target was so large in my sight that the bombs couldn't miss. I pulled the airplane up sharply to avoid further AA fire, and just in case there were enemy fighters around, I took cover in the lower cloud layer.

'The *Fanshaw Bay* had been hit

Final moments of *Zuikaku*, the last surviving carrier of the Pearl Harbor strike force. The Avenger paralleling the target's port beam was one of many that helped sink the ship, and three light carriers off Cape Engano, on 25 October. However, while TF-38 was destroying the remainder of Japan's carrier fleet, Vice Adm Kurita's Centre Force had reversed course and pounced upon Seventh Fleet light units off the east coast of Samar, adding another element to the battle (*Grumman*)

Back aboard *San Jacinto*, VT-51 pilots hold a hurried flightdeck conference. They are discussing what they saw and did over the Ozawa force north-east of Luzon, little knowing that their success had opened the gate to vulnerable American shipping farther south (*National Archives*)

Lt Cdr Edward J Huxtable (left), skipper of VC-10 aboard the escort carrier *Gambier Bay*, poses with his crewmen, AOM1/c R S Martin (centre) and ARM1/c D R Blaney (right). Surprised by the appearance of Japanese battleships and cruisers in Leyte Gulf, VC-10 and the other squadrons of 'Taffy Three' immediately launched with any ordnance available. Huxtable made numerous 'dry runs' against enemy warships, attempting to distract the gunners, and though *Gambier Bay* was sunk, along with three of the destroyer escorts, the threat was repulsed (*Author's collection*)

by surface fire, and aircraft aloft were instructed to proceed to Tacloban Airfield, on the island of Leyte. Just then the Japanese force broke off the engagement and steamed north. The sturdy TBM touched down on a rough runway and braked to a halt one foot from a bomb crater. A ground crewman signalled cut engine. Inspection of the aircraft produced a surprise. Practically every inspection plate had been blown off! But even with these missing plates and canopy, the aircraft remained flyable. Later, a non-flyable TBM was found and much-needed parts were cannibalised.

'At dawn the next day, I gave up my foxhole to the army engineers, relieved that an expected banzai charge had not materialised. Soon my TBM and I were headed east to land on the wet deck of an alternate carrier, where we belonged.'

One of *Gambier Bay's* crews who got ashore was that led by Lt(jg) R L Crocker. His turret gunner, AMM2/c Charles Westbrook, recalled;

'That morning off Samar, Mr Crocker and I were in the third TBM to leave the deck after the attack started. The radioman was a fill-in from another crew which didn't have a plane. We had only four rockets and our guns, but we pressed home what amounted to almost a dummy run in an attempt to divert the enemy ships from our force.

'Mr Crocker started a run on a cruiser, but it turned away so he shifted to a destroyer. He waited until his tracers were bouncing off the deck, then let fly with the rockets. I fired off a full can of ammo on the run. We didn't stick around after that. When we landed on a field south of Tacloban, on Leyte, we found seven holes in the cowling and a 20 mm hole in the port wing. But it really didn't matter, for after we landed, a Wildcat came in on top of us and destroyed both planes. We got out without a scratch.'

The lopsided battle off Samar should have ended in the annihilation of 'Taffy Three'. Instead, the exceptionally determined attacks by Sprague's aircraft and destroyers, backed by aeroplanes from 'Taffy Two', forced the Japanese battle squadron to retire. Gunfire had sunk *Gambier Bay* and three US destroyers, whilst *St Lo* was destroyed by a *kamikaze*. But three of Kurita's fast cruisers had been crippled and left behind to sink – largely due to the efforts of TBM bombs and torpedoes. The threat to MacArthur's invasion force was over.

However, the CVE squadrons had taken a beating. Forty-two TBMs had been lost, either shot down, crashed or sunk with their ships. Including the fast carrier squadrons, which wrote off a dozen more, a record 54 Avengers succumbed to combat or operational attrition on 25 October. Thankfully, aircrew casualties were relatively light, but even when human and materiel losses were heavy, in the ledger of war, the US Navy could absorb the attrition and replace it in kind. Japan could not.

FOUR CARRIERS SUNK

Meanwhile, Lt Taylor's *Independence* Avengers had also found another major enemy force. Two VT(N)-41 TBMs discovered Vice Adm Jisaburo Ozawa's four surviving carriers north-east of Luzon, prompting Halsey to send Task Force 38 racing north, leaving the Seventh Fleet vulnerable to Kurita.

In four major strikes during the 25th, the air groups of TF-38 deprived the Imperial Navy of most of its remaining carriers. Avenger squadrons played a major role in this action, helping sink four carriers and a destroyer. The most successful strike was conducted by Air Groups 19 and 44 off *Lexington* and *Langley*, respectively. During the third attack of the day, TBMs of VT-19 and -44 put three torpedoes into the previously damaged *Zuikaku*. Those 'torpeckers' finished off the veteran of every carrier battle except Midway, and last surviving 'flattop' from the Pearl Harbor strike force. Light carrier *Zuiho* was sunk by elements of five air groups shortly thereafter. Two other CVLs – *Chitose* and *Chiyoda* – also succumbed to the combined might of Task Force 38.

As always, there was a price for victory. A VT-44 crew from the 1145 mission made a water landing near the Japanese task force after the attack, and were reported by their *Langley* shipmates as afloat in a raft. The

destroyer *Hatsuzuki* was assigned rescue duty in the area of the action and picked up a few Japanese fighter pilots, as well as the crew of 44-T-3. *Hatsukzuki* was then intercepted by Halsey's cruisers and destroyers and sunk. Ironically, the Torpedo 44 crew was lost along with the Japanese pilots so recently saved. The *Langley* fliers were Lt William F Doherty, ARM3/c John J Burke and AMM3/c Samuel M. Martin. Their aircraft was TBM-1C BuNo 46053, side number T-3.

During the Ozawa strikes on the 25th, 11 TBM-1Cs were lost, including one VT-44 operational loss during catapult launch when the torpedo shifted and the aircraft could not be controlled properly. After attempts to gain control, the crew finally parachuted and was rescued.

In a bizarre episode, the crash impact resulted in the Avenger's torpedo going active and dispersing several destroyers, which scurried out of the way. This torpedo going 'live' after crashing is near-identical to the Santa Cruz incident of 1942, which resulted in the loss of USS *Porter*!

Of the other losses, four pilots and eight aircrew were killed with the TBMs. Losses (including five that were jettisoned) were from VT-13 (one), VT-15 (one), VT-18 (one), VT-19 (three), VT-20 (one), VT-44 (three) and VT-51 (one).

VT-15 lost 16 aircraft from June through to October 1944, and two more on the final day of operations, 5 November. The last of these was this aircraft, BuNo 46353, which sustained heavy battle damage during a mission over Luzon. The pilot landed safely aboard, but the turret gunner was already dead, and the decision was made to bury the airman and his aircraft at sea. In the second phot, BuNo 46353 has just been pushed off the flightdeck after the completion of a funeral service conducted by a chaplain standing on the wing (*Grumman*)

TO JAPAN

Other than the unique Doolittle Raid of April 1942, no carrier strikes were launched against the Japanese home islands until February 1945, when the two-day operation, flown in poor weather on the 16th and 17th, proved a harbinger of things to come. The 14 fast carriers brought 201 Avengers to the shores of Japan, including new TBM-3s in five air groups.

Tokyo Strikes, 16-17 February 1945

Task Force 38

VT-3	*Yorktown* (CV 10)	18 TBM-1C
VT-4	*Essex* (CV 9)	18 TBM-1C
VT-7	*Hancock* (CV 19)	18 TBM-1C
VT-11	*Hornet* (CV 12)	18 TBM-1C
VT-20	*Lexington* (CV 16)	15 TBM-1C
VT-22	*Cowpens* (CVL 25)	9 TBM-1C
VT-28	*Monterey* (CVL 26)	9 TBM-1C
VT-29	*Cabot* (CVL 28)	9 TBM-1C
VT(N)-41	*Independence* (CVL 22)	8 TBM-1D/-3D
VT-44	*Langley* (CVL 27)	9 TBM-1C/-3/-3P
VT-45	*San Jacinto* (CVL 30)	9 TBM-1C/-3
VT-80	*Ticonderoga* (CV 14)	16 TBM-1C/-3/-3P
VT-81	*Wasp* (CV 18)	18 TBM-1C
VT(N)-90	*Enterprise* (CV 6)	27 TBM-3D

Poor weather hampered strike operations, and the majority of combat revolved around heavy fighter action on the 16th and 17th. However, Avengers were active on both days, and Task Force 38 lost ten to all causes. Meanwhile, escort carriers supporting the Iwo Jima landings wrote off five more.

NIGHT FLIERS

During 1945, three/four new night air groups reported to the Fast Carrier Task Force. There was little commonality in the organisation of each, as the night carrier fraternity had not yet evolved toward that degree of standardisation. However, the most long-lived was Cdr Bill Martin's Air Group 90, embarked in *Enterprise* at the end of 1944. It was Martin's third deployment in 'The Big E', and arguably the most successful, as he explains;

The first major carrier operation of 1945 was a strike against Japanese and Vichy French facilities along the Indochina coast. On 12 January TF-38 conducted the first Allied naval foray into the East China Sea in nearly three years, sinking a French cruiser, hostile merchantmen and razing enemy airfields. Seven TBMs were lost. This VT-20 Avenger off *Lexington* flies past burning tankers in Camn Ranh Bay (*Author's collection*)

'We felt that at night we weren't going to get shot down by anti-aircraft fire, and certainly not by Japanese fighters. Since the TBM gunners weren't needed at night, we tried to get all the defensive stuff taken out, including all the armour plate, except for one plate behind the pilot. We figured that by removing the turret we saved about 1500 lb of unnecessary weight, and we took out the .30-cal "stinger" in the belly. With this weight saving we could put two big fuel tanks in the bomb bay and still have ordnance in the other half. By this time we were also able to carry 5-in rockets under the wings, so we had a pretty good ordnance load, and also enough fuel to go a lot farther.

'The pilot had a radar scope in his cockpit but the main search set was in the belly, facing forward, with two operators. We found we needed two men to spell each other, because on a long mission, after about 20 minutes of looking at the radar, your eyes could get fatigued.

'Our requests to get these aircraft modified prior to the cruise were repeatedly turned down. So with about ten days to go, I flew over to see the highest level possible at Ford Island, Pearl Harbor, and got all the way up to Vice Adm John H Towers. He told me, "Our engineers have studied this thing, and the airplane won't fly the way you want to use it". What he didn't know was that we had worked all night before in VT(N)-90 to do the modification. So I told Adm Towers, "If it won't fly, sir, I request a jeep to take me back to Barbers Point because I flew a modified TBM over here, and if it won't fly, I sure don't want to fly it back!"'

Independence had concluded her nocturnal deployment with Cdr Caldwell's Air Group 41, and reverted to conventional daylight operations in early 1945. But *Saratoga* embarked a mixed complement in Air Group 53, with dedicated day and night squadrons, affording round-the-clock support of the Iwo Jima operation in February. The Avengers of VT(N)-53 worked well for five consecutive days and nights, but 'Sara' was nearly destroyed by four suicide hits on 21 February. *Enterprise* took up the slack for the next week, flying 53 per cent of all sorties after dark with only two operational losses.

Martin's TBM-3Ds, led by Lt Russell Kippen, engaged in a

Torpedo Squadron Four, which more than a year earlier had sunk German-controlled ships in Norway, found itself over Indochina on 12 January 1945. *Essex* markings were little changed from Air Group 15, although three-digit side numbers were becoming increasingly common in the Fast Carrier Task Force (*Author's collection*)

Composite Squadron 76 was the 'plankowner' unit aboard the escort carrier *Petrof Bay*. This TBM-1C (BuNo 73495) was flown by Lt(jg) Rothwell, with aircrewmen AMM2/c Cain and ARM2/c Henning. The aircraft was named *'Blopsy'* after the pilot's wife, and carried a figure of cartoon character *Betty Boop* forward of the VC-76 emblem (*Larry Coté*)

variety of missions, including some of carrier aviation's earliest electronic countermeasures operations. In mid-May the Avengers attacked Japanese air and naval bases on Kyushu, but on the 14th a *kamikaze* dived into *Enterprise's* forward elevator. The resulting explosion knocked the veteran carrier out of the war. Kippen's squadron had sunk two enemy ships, probably sank two more, and damaged about 30. Besides nearly 100 tons of bombs, the TBMs had launched just one torpedo, but the night-riding Avengers proved surprising effective at night air combat. The squadron claimed five shootdowns, including two each by Lt(jg) Charles E Henderson III and Lt(jg) Clifton R Largess. Henderson also claimed a probable with VT(N)-90, and had previously downed a 'Jill' with VT-10, thus making him the most successful Avenger pilot in air-to-air combat.

Of nine night torpedo squadrons established during World War 2, only four deployed to combat. The last was VT(N)-91, which cameaboard the *Essex*-class carrier *Bon Homme Richard* in June of 1945 and was still in combat on VJ-Day.

ECM

By this stage of the war, chaff was regularly employed by carrier

Among the new squadrons committed to combat in early 1945 was *Bennington's* VT-82. This TBM-3 makes a deck-run takeoff beneath leaden skies and in choppy seas during February operations leading up to the first series of strikes against the Japanese home islands. The overall gloss blue finish became increasingly common on TBMs at this point of the war as the tri-colour scheme was gradually phased out (*Author's collection*)

'Love Day' at Okinawa was 1 April 1945, with the heavy commitment of the fast carriers and the dedicated close air support skills of the CVEs. The flightdeck of *Rudyerd Bay* shows VC-96 Avengers and Wildcats with their distinctive 'tic-tac-toe' emblem, but not quite standard colour schemes or aircraft numbers. Most are overall gloss blue, with at least two TBMs still bearing the tri-colour scheme and one Wildcat minus the usual tail number (*Author's collection*)

bombers to jam enemy radars. For instance, the Avengers of VT-84 conducted electronic countermeasures experiments during strike missions over Japan. Active (as opposed to passive) jamming was conducted electronically by AN/APT-1 sets, and one aeroplane in most flights also carried AN/APR-1 and -11 radar receivers and analysers. Post-mission analysis permitted onboard jammers to be retuned if the analysers detected radar operating outside the normal band-width.

SINKING *YAMATO*

On 7 April 1945 the Imperial Japanese Navy launched its last seaborne offensive of the war. The huge battleship *Yamato*, escorted by a light cruiser and a squadron of destroyers, sortied with enough fuel to reach Okinawa, where the armada was expected to perish after inflicting substantial damage on the US invasion fleet.

Despite poor weather, Task Force 58 aircraft tracked the ten Japanese warships throughout the day. Vice Adm Mitscher's flagship, USS *Bunker Hill*, operated Air Group 84 under Cdr Roger E Hedrick, who led the 300-aeroplane strike.

Low ceilings and limited visibility hampered the search, but eventually the *Yamato* force was found approximately 270 miles from TF-58. *Bunker Hill's* base element was composed of Lt Cdr John Conn's SB2C Helldivers, which gained radar contact at 32 nautical miles. The target became visible at about 20 miles, but low clouds prevented a co-ordinated attack. The bombers selected a destroyer and sent it down stern first.

Meanwhile, Lt Cdr Chandler Swanson's VT-84 conducted its first all-torpedo attack. Swanson had flown TBDs at Coral Sea, and was well experienced in the theory and practice of dealing with capital ships. He briefed his pilots;

'We will go after the battleship – nothing else. Our torpedoes are set for the proper depth. This is our target.'

The skipper split his 14 aircraft, eight attacking from port and six from starboard. Driving through heavy flak at 200 to 700 ft, they boxed in the 64,000-ton giant, but one plane was shot down during the run-in. Lt(jg) R J Walsh, ARM2/c G E Heath and AMM2/c

Score one for Japanese flak gunners on Okinawa. This VT-83 TBM heads for a water landing minus most of its horizontal stabiliser – it was one of four aircraft lost by the squadron during April. Air Group 83 had relieved Air Group 4 aboard *Essex* in early March, and remained aboard the veteran carrier until the end of hostilities some five months later (*Author's collection*)

Individual aircraft names were rare among Avenger squadrons, but *DoT* belonged to VT-40, part of Air Group 40, aboard the escort carrier *Suwannee*. The TBM-3 is seen here patrolling near Okinawa on 27 April 1945. The placement of the aircraft number 87 below the rudder is fairly unusual (*Author's collection*)

Ground support has always been the *sine qua non* of Marine Corps aviation, no less in World War 2 than anytime since. These two gloss blue TBMs belong to VMTB-233, embarked in the second *Block Island* (CVE 106) during the Okinawa campaign in May 1945. The nearest Avenger, No 57, is probably a replacement aircraft, since it has not yet received the unmistakable 'Block I' tail emblem of No 53 (*Author's collection*)

Among the oldest squadrons in the Marine Corps was VMTB-232, the famous 'Red Devils', dating from the 1920s. This trio formed up for the camera in June 1945, bearing the traditional devil in a small diamond on the vertical stabiliser. All three TBMs have the standard three-digit number forward of the 'star and bar', this usually duplicating the Bureau of Aeronautics serial, but the gloss blue lead aircraft has a non-standard '277' forward of the wing root as well (*Author's collection*)

C V Whiteman were killed and another TBM was badly damaged, but the unit pressed on. Nine crews claimed hits on the target, slamming seven torpedoes into her port side and two from starboard.

Other air groups were stacked up, awaiting their turn. Eventually, a total of 19 torpedo hits was claimed upon *Yamato*, but the huge warship was no easy prey. She was still afloat as the strike leader turned his Corsair for home.

When Hedrick returned to CV 17, he reported all but three destroyers sunk in perhaps the largest war-at-sea strike in naval aviation history. At 1600 came word that *Yamato* had capsized and exploded. The VT-84 history called it 'the highlight of the combat tour.'

Belleau Wood's air group also relished the opportunity. Air Group 30 reported;

'As the planes began their attack, the big battlewagon and her escorts unloosed a barrage of AA fire with every available weapon, including the heavy guns of their main batteries!

'One of our torpedo planes, piloted by Lt(jg) Ernie Delaney, was hit by AA during his run on the *Yamato*. The entire crew parachuted, but only the pilot survived. Edward J Mawhinney and William Tilley were never seen again. For four hours by his lift raft, Delaney watched the drama of a dying Jap task group five miles away. A destroyer approached to within 400 yards of him – then suddenly turned away – perhaps thinking the raft was unoccupied since Ernie was in the water, concealing himself. When two PBMs flew over, Delaney climbed into the raft to wave wildly for recognition. One PBM swung off, drawing the fire of the Jap force, which had observed what was going on; the other landed and taxied by the raft. Fed, (*text continues on page 61*)

COLOUR PLATES

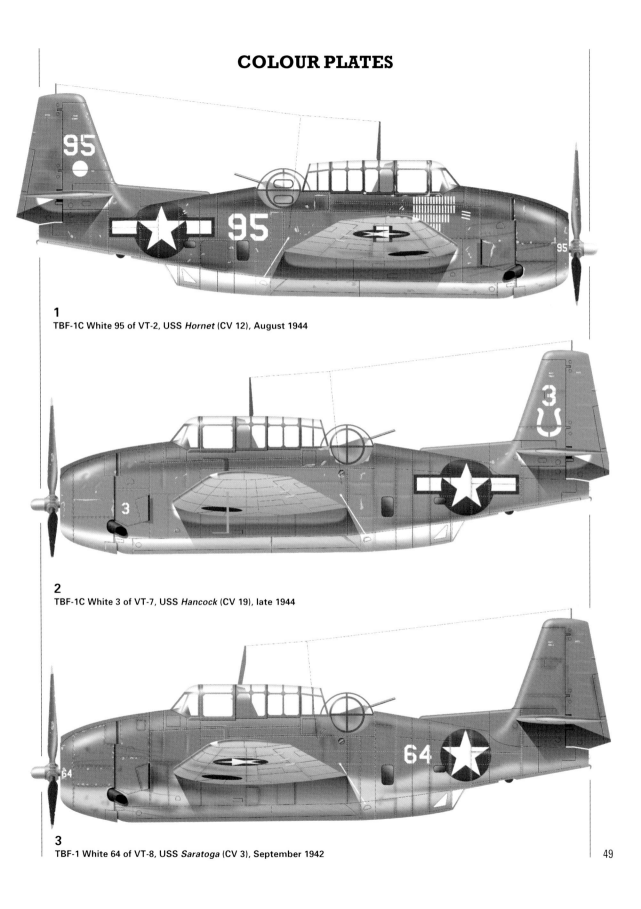

1
TBF-1C White 95 of VT-2, USS *Hornet* (CV 12), August 1944

2
TBF-1C White 3 of VT-7, USS *Hancock* (CV 19), late 1944

3
TBF-1 White 64 of VT-8, USS *Saratoga* (CV 3), September 1942

4
TBM-3 White 22 of VC-8, USS *Nehenta Bay* (CVE 74), February 1945

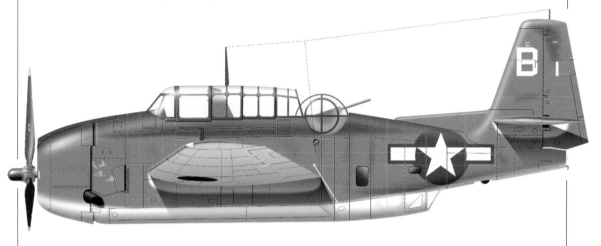

5
TBM-1C White B1 of VC-10, flown by unit CO, Lt Cdr E J Huxtable, USS *Gambier Bay* (CVE 73), October 1944

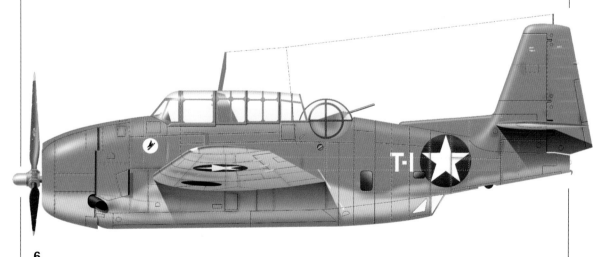

6
TBF-1 White T-1 of VT-10, flown by unit CO, Lt Cdr W I Martin, USS *Enterprise* (CV 6), late 1943

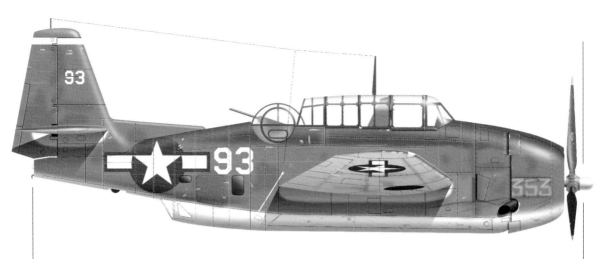

7
TBF-1C White 93 of VT-15, USS *Essex* (CV 9), November 1944

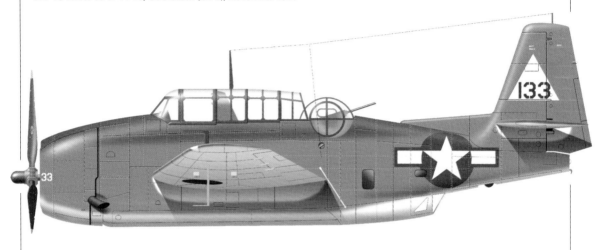

8
TBM-3 White 133 of VT-20, USS *Lexington* (CV 16), January 1945

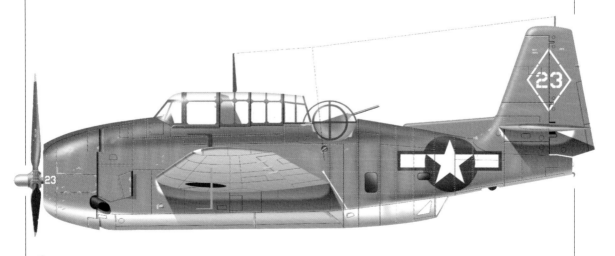

9
TBM-1C BuNo 46203 White 23 of VC-21, USS *Marcus Island* (CVE 77), August 1944

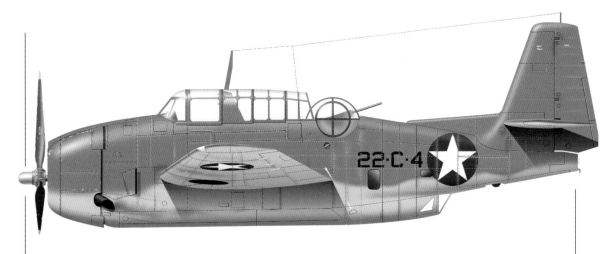

10
TBF-1 Black 22-C-4 of VC-22, USS *Independence* (CVL 22), May 1943

11
TBF-1C White 9 of VT-24, flown by Lt(jg) Warren Omark, USS *Belleau Wood* (CVL 24), June 1944

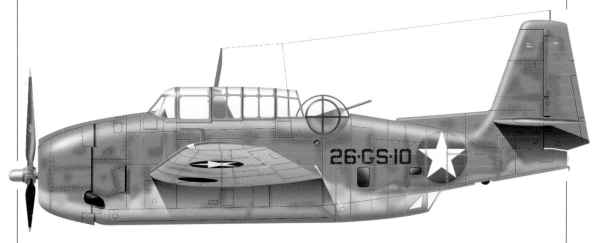

12
TBF-1 Black 26-GS-10 of VGS-26, USS *Charger* (CVE 30), late 1942

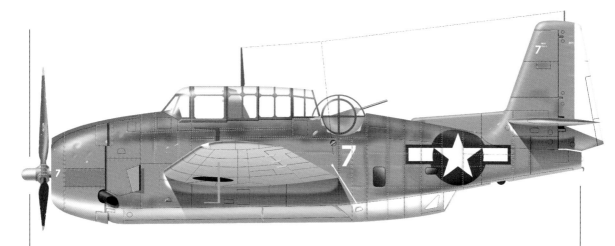

13
TBF-1C White 7 of VT-31, USS *Cabot* (CVL 28), July 1944

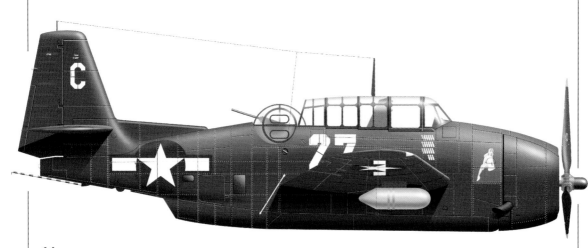

14
TBM-3E White 27 of VT-34, USS *Monterey* (CVL 26), July 1945

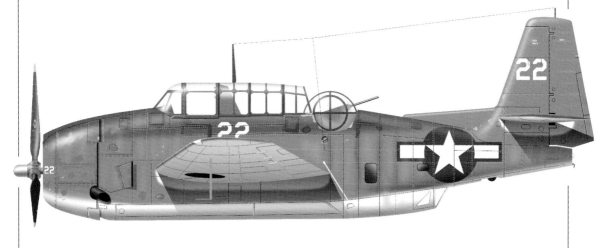

15
TBM-1D White 22 of VT(N)-41, USS *Independence* (CVL 22), October 1944

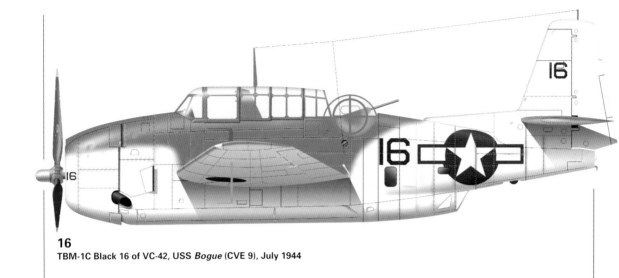

16
TBM-1C Black 16 of VC-42, USS *Bogue* (CVE 9), July 1944

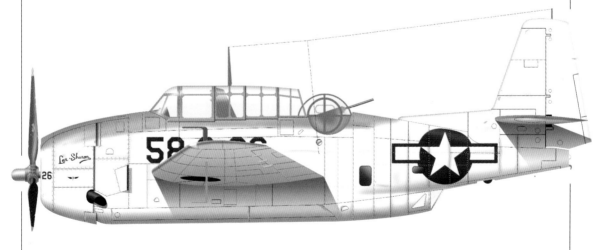

17
TBM-1C White 51-T-8 of VT-51, USS *San Jacinto* (CVL 30), February 1944

18

TBF-1C Black 58-C-26 *Len-Sharon* of VC-58, USS *Block Island* (CVE 21), January 1944

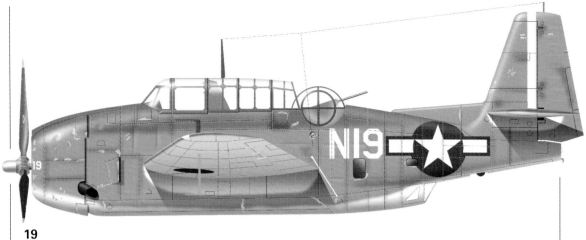

19
TBF-1C White N19 of VC-63, USS *Natoma Bay* (CVE 62), February 1944

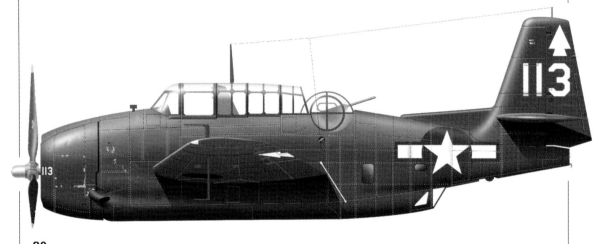

20
TBM-3 White 113 of VT-82, USS *Bennington* (CV 20), February 1945

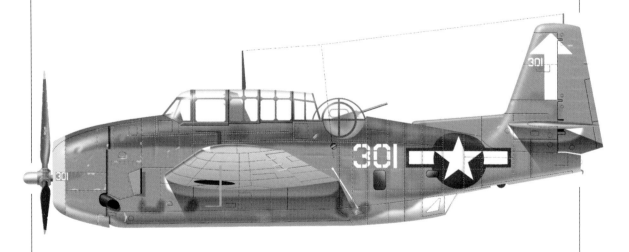

21
TBM-3 White 301 of VT-84, USS *Bunker Hill* (CV 17), February 1945

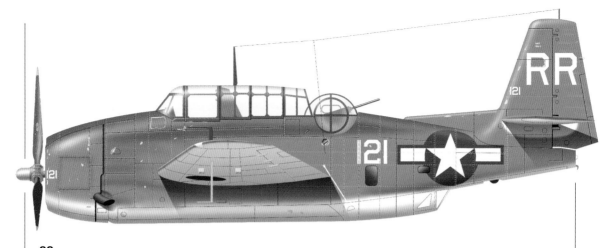

22
TBM-3 White 121 of VT-88, USS *Yorktown* (CV 10), August 1945

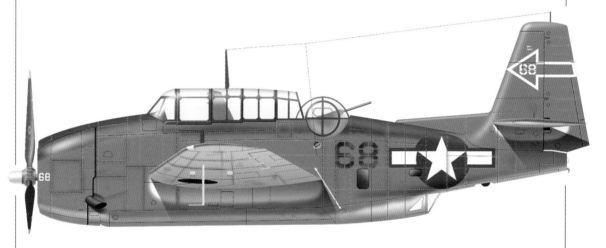

23
TBM-3D White/Black 68 of VT(N)-90, USS *Enterprise* (CV 6), early 1945

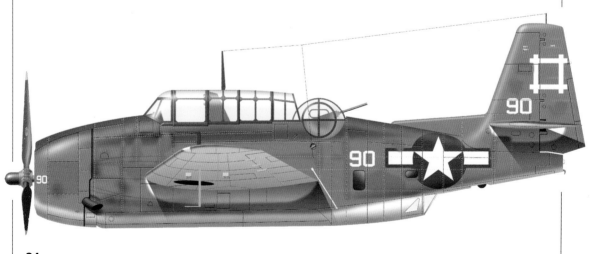

24
TBM-3 White 90 of VC-96, USS *Rudyerd Bay* (CVE 81), April 1945

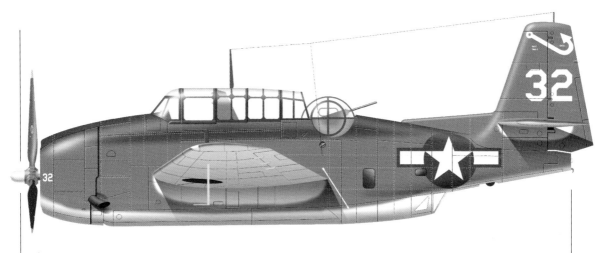

25
TBM-3 White 32 of VC-97, USS *Makassar Strait* (CVE 91), March 1945

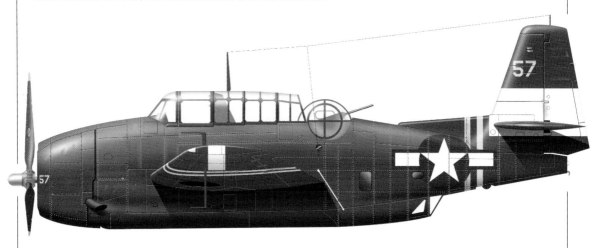

26
TBM-3 Yellow 57 of VMTB-132, USS *Cape Gloucester* (CVE 109), July 1945

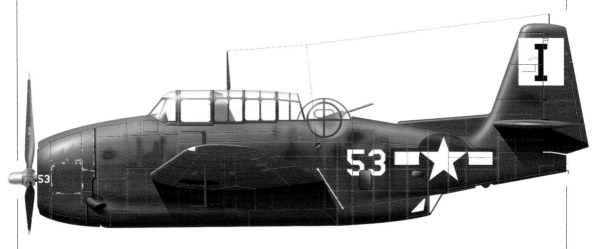

27
TBM-3 White 53 of VMTB-233, USS *Block Island* (CVE 106), May 1945

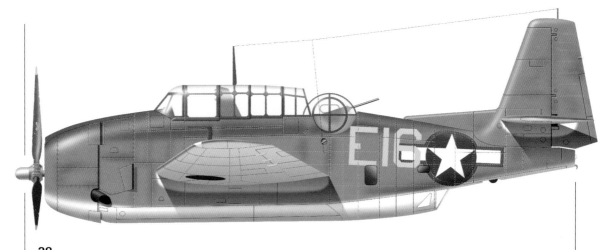

28
TBF-1C Yellow E16 of an unidentified Operational Training Unit, USS *Mission Bay* (CVE 59), November 1943

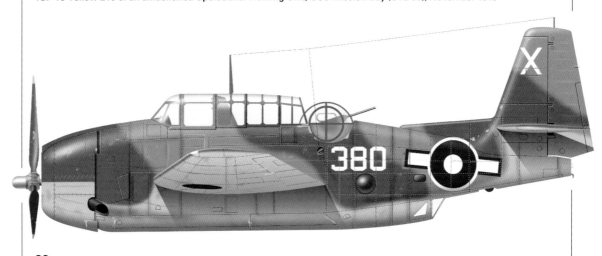

29
Avenger II JZ466 White 380 of No 848 Sqn, HMS *Formidable* (67), August 1945

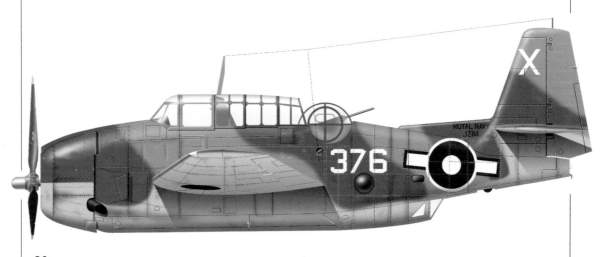

30
Avenger I JZ114 of No 848 Sqn, HMS *Formidable* (67), August 1945

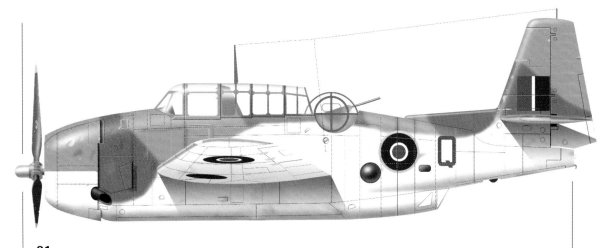

31
Avenger II Red Q of No 853 Sqn, HMS *Queen*, April 1945

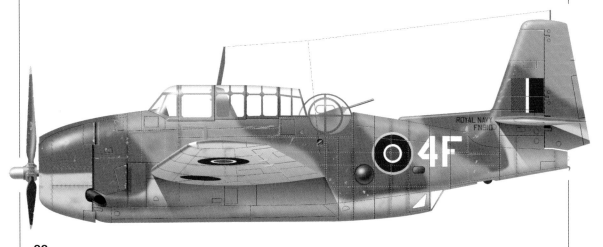

32
Tarpon I FN910 White 4F of No 846 Sqn, Macrihanish, Scotland, December 1943

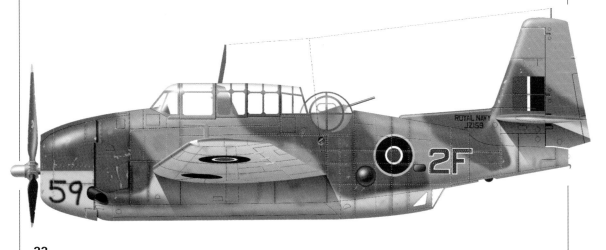

33
Avenger I JZ159 Red 2F/Black 59 of No 852 Sqn, HMS *Nabob*, early 1944

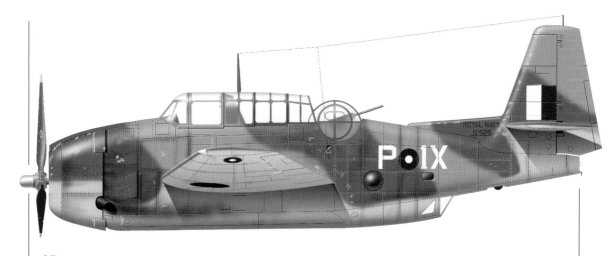

35
Avenger II JZ525 White P1X of No 849 Sqn, HMS *Victorious* (38), January 1945

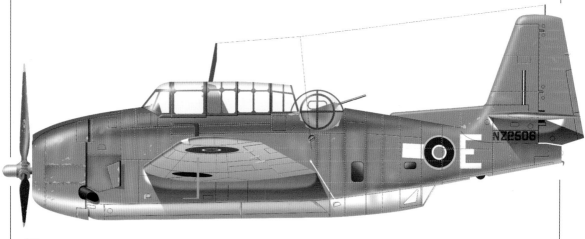

35
TBF-1C NZ2506 White E of No 30 Sqn, Piva, early 1944

36
TBF-1C NZ2518 White 518 of No 30 Sqn, flown by Flt Lt Fred Ladd, Piva, May 1944

'The war must go on'. A VC-9 TBM-3E is catapulted from *Natoma Bay* even as repairs continue on the forward edge of the flightdeck. This photo was taken on 7 June, just 24 hours after a *kamikaze* had struck the 'jeep' carrier. Despite these deadly attacks, Task Force 52 continued operations unabated in the Ryukyus, sending strikes and patrols over Okinawa and Sakashima (*Author's collection*)

This spectacular photo attests to the quality of products from the 'Eastern Division of Grumman Iron Works'. This VT-82 TBM lost half its port wing and most of the fuselage decking between the turret and its tail, yet kept flying long enough to make a successful ditching. In part, the Avenger's large wing area enabled the rugged airframe to sustain adequate lift despite severe damage – a quality much beloved by aircrew (*Liberator Club*)

clothed and bandaged by her crew, Ernie asked for news of his crewmen. But the PBM pilot, who had thoroughly searched the area, reported seeing no trace of them. Low fuel prevented a further search.'

The *Yamato* strike, which destroyed the battleship, a light cruiser and four destroyers, was an unqualified success, but not without losses. Official records state that three Hellcats, four Helldivers and three Avengers were lost. However, five more TBMs were jettisoned with extensive damage upon return to their ships. Avengers were lost by VT-17 (two, including one in the target area), VT-30 (one in the target area), VT-47 (one), VT-82 (one), and VT-84 (three – one in the target area). Two pilots and six aircrew were lost, as at this time most squadrons flew with one 'airdale', either the radioman or gunner.

HOME ISLANDS

As the Pacific war came closer to the Japanese home islands, the intensity of operations predictably increased. Already known as a ruthlessly tenacious enemy, the Japanese redoubled their efforts to defend not only their homeland, but what they regarded as sacred soil. The result was a tempo and ferocity of air-sea combat previously unknown.

For Avenger squadrons, now equipped almost entirely with TBMs, the opportunity for anti-shipping missions declined rapidly. However, overland strikes and anti-submarine patrols kept torpedo squadrons fully occupied, and attrition remained high. Typically, 100 or more Avengers were lost or stricken each month.

Bunker Hill's VT-84 sustained heavier than usual losses for a TorpRon at this phase of the war. Between mid-February and mid-May the squadron lost four aircraft operationally, one to flak and two downed by Japanese fighters. However, on 11 May a *kamikaze* inflicted crippling injuries on the ship and her air group: most of the aeroplanes aboard were destroyed,

A 'mix and match' colour scheme is evident on *Saginaw Bay's* rocket-armed TBM-3s in the summer of 1945. Both Avengers bear the familiar tri-colour scheme, but the lead aircraft has a replacement tail in gloss blue – a striking background for the double lightning bolts. Note that '86' also has a fuselage number oversprayed forward of the national marking, indicating that it was perhaps transferred in from another carrier (*Author's collection*)

but the human cost was staggering. *Bunker Hill* lost 389 dead or missing and 264 wounded – figures only exceeded by *Franklin's* horrific casualties in a conventional bombing attack in March.

Air Group 84 lost 103 of the *Bunker Hill* fatalities, including 26 officers and men of VT-84 – far more than had died in combat flying. All 15 of the squadrons TBM-3s were also were consumed in the raging fires on the flight and hangar decks.

With the Japanese fleet lying 'doggo' in home ports, the need for torpedoes diminished further than before. Consequently, most TBM missions in the final weeks of the war were flown with bombs or mines. VT-30's mission of 18 July was typical;

'*Belleau Wood* launched a strike of eight fighters and nine torpedo bombers to participate with other task force aircraft in an attack on the *Nagato*. Photographic intelligence showed this target to be well camouflaged at a Yokosuka dock. Since this area was a hotbed of AA

Another mixed batch of early- and late-production TBM-3s, this time from *Yorktown's* Torpedo 88 in late August. Their RR tail code replaced the previous air group marking, which featured a diagonal white division of the vertical stabiliser and rudder. Air Group 88 was involved in the last aerial combat in Japanese airspace when a division of Hellcats was attacked just after receiving the recall order from the task force (*Author's collection*)

Why is this pilot smiling? He must have known when this photograph was taken on 29 August that the formal Japanese surrender was just four days off. Hailing from *Monterey's* VT-34, the lead aircraft in this stepped-down echelon formation is a late model TBM-3E. It is unusual by 1945 standards in that it bears both mission markers (21 bombs) and a sultry *'Petty Girl'* painted on the engine access panel behind the cowling (*Author's collection*)

The last wartime carrier to reach the Western Pacific was *Antietam* (CV 36), embarking the TBM-3s of TorpRon 89. Seen airborne over Shanghai, this Avenger retains earlier 'G' symbols on its tail and ailerons, rather than an assigned letter (*Author's collection*)

positions, the torpedo planes were loaded with 260-lb fragmentation bombs for neutralising the anti-aircraft positions, while the fighters were to bomb the ship with 1000-pounders.

'The "Beaulah's" planes went in on the third wave. By this time planes were coming in from all directions, and smoke from exploding bombs had completely obscured the *Nagato*. Anti-aircraft fire, as expected, was intense, and necessitated violent evasive tactics. What

with dodging friendly planes, ducking enemy AA and trying to bomb through smoke as thick as pea soup, the pilots couldn't be assured of much accuracy, nor could they stay around to check the results. The mighty battlewagon did not receive a fatal blow, nor in fact as severe damage as was originally reported.'

A subsequent strike against Kure Harbour on 24 July repeated the process, with TBMs directed against the defences while F6Fs delivered bombs against the battleship *Ise*. Damage was inflicted on the immobile ship, preventing any chance of her getting underway.

During the last two weeks of hostilities, Avengers were active both over Japanese soil and in adjoining waters. Fifty TBMs were lost, including more than 20 pool aircraft retired in Hawaii and the Philippines. Among fleet squadrons, the last four recorded losses occurred on 13 August, with one each from VT-1 aboard *Bennington*, VT-85 embarked in *Shangri-La*, VT-87 in *Ticonderoga* and VC-41 aboard *Makin Island*.

A peacetime 'trap.' This colourfully marked TBM engages the last arresting wire on *Petrof Bay* on 9 September 1945. By that time the world had been at peace for one week, and the navy was already putting into place plans to hastily decommission most of its carriers and disestablish the majority of its squadrons and air groups (*Author's collection*)

Avenger Squadrons Against Japan, VJ-Day

Task Force 38

VT-1	*Bennington* (CV 20)	12 TBM-3/3E
VT-6	*Hancock* (CV 19)	15 TBM-3E
VT-16	*Randolph* (CV 15)	15 TBM-3/3E
VT-27	*Independence* (CVL 22)	9 TBM-3/3E
VT-31	*Belleau Wood* (CVL 24)	9 TBM-3/3E
VT-34	*Monterey* (CVL 26)	12 TBM-3/3P
VT-47	*Bataan* (CVL 29)	9 TBM-3E
VT-49	*San Jacinto* (CVL 30)	9 TBM-3
VT-50	*Cowpens* (CVL 25)	9 TBM-3E
VT-83	*Essex* (CV 9)	15 TBM-3/3E
VT-85	*Shangri-La* (CV 38)	15 TBM-3E
VT-86	*Wasp* (CV 18)	15 TBM-3E
VT-87	*Ticonderoga* (CV 14)	15 TBM-3E
VT-88	*Yorktown* (CV 10)	15 TBM-3/3E
VT(N)-91	*Bon Homme Richard* (CV 31)	17 TBM-3E
VT-94	*Lexington* (CV 16)	15 TBM-3E
No 820 Sqn	HMS *Indefatigable* (10)	20 Avenger II

Escort Carrier Force

VC-66	*Anzio* (CVE 57)	9 TBM-3/3E/3P
VC-70	*Salamaua* (CVE 70)	9 TBM-3E
VMTB-132	*Cape Gloucester* (CVE 109)	9 TBM-3E
VMTB-143	*Gilbert Islands* (CVE 107)	9 TBM-3E

SUB HUNTER

The 'Atlantic Gap' was a dreadful fact of life for Allied merchant-men during most of World War 2. Despite long-range patrol aircraft based in Newfoundland, in Iceland and the British Isles, there still existed a 500- to 1200-mile stretch along the North Atlantic convoy routes beyond air cover. Not even British acquisition of bases in the Azores in late 1943 significantly closed what merchant sailors called the 'Black Pit'. In this area, German U-boats preyed off Allied convoys without fear of air attack . . . until the spring of 1943.

At the end of 1941 the US Maritime Commission released 20 freighter hulls for conversion to escort aircraft carriers, or CVEs. Ten went to the US Navy and ten to Britain. They were followed by four converted tankers, and then by the 50-ship *Casablanca* class, which were all built from the keel up as carriers. Despite these various classes, all CVEs were approximately similar – an overall length of 500-550 ft, top speed of 17-19 knots and capable of operating up to 30 aircraft.

By early March 1943 the first American submarine hunter-killer unit was operational. This was the *Bogue* group, composed of four ex-World War 1 destroyers grouped around the first American CVE employed in convoy escort. *Bogue* embarked Composite Squadron Nine (VC-9) under Lt Cdr William M Drane, and initially flew eight TBF-1s and a dozen F4F-4s. The Avenger was immediately recognised as a natural for such work. Its range, endurance and payload made it ideally suited to both search and

A bad way to start the day: a depth bomb explodes off a U-boat's starboard beam, while another just enters the water 25 ft from the hull. Two crewmen are visible on deck, having abandoned the 37 mm gun on the mount aft of the conning tower. Although the submarine is unidentified, the date is probably the latter half of 1943 (*Author's collection*)

A TBF circles low over the spot where it has depth-bombed a German submarine. Often, accurate assessment of such an attack was impossible until captured enemy records were available for comparison with US or British documents after the war. Subsequent analysis credited US Avengers with more than 30 submarine kills in the Atlantic, and Royal Navy aircraft with three more (*Author's collection*)

strike roles in hunting German submarines.

And there were plenty to hunt. In March Adm Karl Doenitz had an average of 116 U-boats at sea each day – one-third on station and two-thirds en route to patrol areas or returning to base for refit. That month they sank 108 merchant ships totalling over 620,000 gross tons. The Battle of the Atlantic was still in doubt.

Bogue escorted three convoys during March and April, with an inauspicious beginning. Heavy seas and poor flying weather cancelled many search missions, and only two U-boats were seen, and neither was attacked.

The U-boat campaign was a year-round enterprise, regardless of weather. These sailors kept warm by shovelling snow from the flightdeck of an escort carrier in the North Atlantic during the winter of 1942-43. With the onset of spring, the hunting would be much improved, and American carrier aircraft began logging their first submarine sinkings (*Grumman*)

But the aerial hunter-killers were learning. Early experience demonstrated that U-boats did in fact have to be actively hunted. Simply maintaining an 'umbrella' over a convoy was small deterrent to a determined U-boat skipper, who could slip in and fire his torpedoes before being spotted. Avenger search patterns were expanded to fan out ahead and on both sides of the convoy, thereby increasing probability of an early contact. The complement was altered to include only nine F4Fs and increased to 12 TBFs, as the latter were more versatile. Search teams generally composed both a Wildcat and an Avenger for flexibility and mutual support.

The new techniques brought results. In the late evening of 21 May *Bogue* was escorting the westbound convoy ON-184 when VC-9's CO, Lt Cdr Drane, spotted a surfaced U-boat 60 miles ahead of the convoy. He pushed his Avenger into a dive on U-231 and made an accurate bombing attack which badly damaged the vessel's bridge. Although the U-boat was not sunk, it was forced to turn east for repair.

'Business' picked up dramatically the next day. Early that morning a TBF found a submarine surfacing 55 miles from *Bogue*. The pilot took advantage of low-lying clouds to conceal his approach, but was seen by the German lookouts and forced to abandon his attack due to heavy AA fire. Communications problems prevented reinforcement aircraft from arriving in time for a co-ordinated attack. At the same time, another TBF sighted a second submarine 35 miles ahead of the convoy and descended to strike, but was foiled when the U-boat 'pulled the plug' and dived while still out of range.

During mid-morning a third U-boat was caught napping by Ens Stewart E Doty, who ruptured its pressure hull with a near-miss by one of four bombs he dropped. This boat, *U-305*, dived to make temporary repairs and surfaced about three hours later only to be pounced upon by another Avenger. Like the first sub, this one considered itself fortunate and shaped course for Brest.

'Third time lucky' had not held true on 23 May, but the fourth contact of the day held the charm. A radio direction finder bearing in the afternoon put U-569 only 20 miles from *Bogue* just as Lt(jg) William F

Chamberlain saw it. He quickly attacked and dropped all four bombs close aboard the U-boat, which crash-dived. The hunters of VC-9 knew they had not sunk the boat, and literally kept on top of it through the rest of the afternoon. When *U-569* surfaced, Lt Howard S Roberts was overhead. He dropped a full spread of four depth charges which did not prevent the vessel from diving, but she had to come up again almost immediately, and was scuttled.

Thus, *U-569* was the first kill made by the US Navy's aerial hunter-killer teams. The first Axis submarine sunk by Avengers had been a Vichy French boat sent to the bottom off Casablanca by three VS-27 TBFs from *Suwannee* during the North African invasion of November 1942. But that was an isolated incident unrelated to the Battle of the Atlantic. *Bogue's* convoy completed its passage without the loss of a single ship, which was in itself remarkable. Some convoys were losing 40 per cent of their merchantmen at this time.

Bogue aircraft sank two more U-boats in June, but the mere tally of sinkings was only a small part of the shifting trend toward eventual victory in the Atlantic. In the last three months of 1942, U-boats sank over 300 merchant ships for nearly 1,800,000 gross tons. In the first quarter of 1943 – the period when CVE aircraft began covering the 'Atlantic Gap' – merchant sinkings dropped to 243. Patrolling Avengers and Wildcats had discouraged many large-scale wolf-pack attacks on escorted convoys by sighting the submarines before they were positioned to strike. The trend continued into the second quarter of 1943, as merchant losses were cut to 150 ships of less than a million tons, while U-boat losses for those three months almost doubled to 73. For the first time the kill-loss ratio of ships to submarines plunged to near parity, at only two-to-one. It had not previously been below six-to-one.

From the escort carriers' viewpoint, July 1943 was the definite turnaround in the campaign. *Core*, with VC-13 embarked, and *Santee*, with VC-29, made their first kills that month which, combined with *Bogue*, accounted for six U-boats. But it was not all one-sided.

When Adm Karl Doenitz, the U-boat commander, learned that carrier aircraft were operating in the North Atlantic, he took quick action. In April he ordered heavier anti-aircraft armament installed on

First blood. Lt Howard S Roberts of *Bogue's* VC-9 dropped four Mk 17 depth bombs from his TBF-1 in this attack on 22 May 1943. Two of the weapons are visible in the right side of the photo. U-569 was sunk, marking the initial success of US hunter-killer tactics. In the previous three days, four contacts had resulted in two attacks and two submarines damaged. CompRon 9 ended the war as the top-rated anti-submarine squadron in the US Navy (*National Archives*)

his boats, and instructed his skippers to stand and fight any aircraft. It took time for these orders to be implemented, but in mid-July Avenger crews began discovering for themselves how formidable the AA defences could be. With four 20 mm guns and a 37 mm, a U-boat could put up a terrific amount of flak.

On the afternoon of 13 July a VC-13 team off *Core* caught the 1600-ton tanker *U-487* on the surface. The F4F dived to strafe and suppress AA fire, but was solidly hit by the automatic weapons and crashed into the ocean. Three more aircraft were summoned to the scene and made a co-ordinated attack, splitting the defences. A TBF got in close enough to drop its bombs, and *U-487* was finished.

Until now, all Avenger ASW kills had been made by bombs or depth charges. But the next day, 14 July, a new weapon was employed. A VC-29 team off Santee sighted *U-160* on the surface that morning, and the Wildcat went down to strafe according to new doctrine. The attack caused the U-boat to dive, which was just what TBF pilot Lt(jg) John Ballentine was hoping for. He dropped his Mk 24 Fido torpedo, which homed on the boat's engines and scored a direct hit. An underwater explosion erupted to the surface, and *U-160* never came back up.

Less than 24 hours later another *Santee* Avenger scored a kill with a Fido. Then, on the 16th, a VC-13 TBF from *Core* destroyed U-67 with a load of bombs. The CVEs had sent four U-boats to the bottom in four consecutive days. *Bogue* and *Santee* Avengers made the last two kills of the month using depth charges and a Fido.

Six more kills came in August, including four by VC-1 aboard *Card*. No sub sinkings were made by CVE aeroplanes in September, but during October, *Card*, *Core* and *Croatan* aircraft executed 20 attacks, claiming 12 kills. In truth 'only' six of these claims were valid, but undoubtedly other U-boats were damaged. The hunter-killer TBFs and F4Fs thought five submarines were destroyed during November, and *Bogue*, with VC-19 now embarked, finished the year with single kills in the last two months of 1943.

American escort carriers sank 23 U-boats from May through to December, nearly all by Avengers.

This excellent photo may have been taken aboard USS *Bogue* in 1944. The Avenger's exhaust stack has been modified with a flame dampener for added security during nocturnal operations, while the FM-2 Wildcat bears no such alterations – surely a good sign for fighter pilots! (*Grumman*)

Submarines were often the lesser enemy, as demonstrated by the rolling deck of this escort carrier running through heavy Atlantic swells. In extreme conditions, the flightdeck could develop 'excursions' of 60 ft or more, making a safe landing all but impossible. (*Grumman*)

As demonstrated by this photo, Grumman/Eastern products owned a monopoly on US Navy anti-submarine carrier aircraft, with Avengers and Wildcats being the 'sole proprietors'. The Atlantic Theatre colour scheme is evident: insignia white overall with gull grey sides and upper surfaces. Barely visible under the airborne TBF's starboard wing is the 1944-style national insignia (*Grumman*)

Working with destroyers and other anti-submarine vessels, they trimmed shipping losses in the last quarter of 1943 to 89 ships of less than half-a-million tons. A year before, it was not unusual to lose that much in a single month. The most successful squadron was VC-9, with eight kills during 1943. Half had been scored while flying from *Bogue* under Lt Cdr Drane, and half from *Card* under Lt Cdr H M Avery. Then the unit served aboard *Solomons* for two months in 1944, still led by Avery, and got a ninth boat. But it was no push over.

On 15 June 1944 a radio direction finding fix indicated a submarine nearby, and Ens George E Edwards 'sniffed it out'. The U-boats still believed in the fight-back policy, and *U-860* shot down Edwards' Avenger before he could get off a position report. A thorough search pattern turned up the troublesome boat again at dusk, when Lt Cdr Avery found *U-860* on the surface. He knew he stood little chance of sinking the vessel unassisted, but astutely judged that it would 'stand and fight'. He kept it occupied with strafing runs for 20 minutes while homing in three other aircraft. Despite the increased odds, *U-860* remained surfaced to shoot it out as darkness fell. Lt(jg) Chamberlain, who had damaged *U-569* in the squadron's first kill over a year before, pressed his attack to point-blank range. His bombs exploded just as he passed overhead, destroying both victor and victim in the blast.

Three months earlier a similar incident had occurred. On 19 March a VC-6 team off *Block Island* found the 'milch cow' *U-1059* early in the morning. Some of the Germans were enjoying a swim when the

This remarkable shot depicts the first US Navy rocket attack against a U-boat. A VC-58 Avenger caught the submarine on the surface, and the trail of two HVARs is clearly visible. A kill was claimed, but postwar records failed to confirm the loss of a U-boat on the date in question – 11 January 1944 (*National Archives*)

Wildcat dived to strafe the sub, but her AA guns were manned immediately and the Avenger was hit during its attack. The TBM pilot, Lt(jg) Norman Dowty, ignored the damage and continued his run. He released two depth bombs, one of which exploded in the sub's ammunition locker, and both TBM and U-boat were destroyed. One of Dowty's crew was rescued, and seven Germans.

That was the only U-boat sunk by *Block Island* aircraft, although the destroyers of her screen sent five subs to the bottom. The *Kriegsmarine* exacted revenge on 29 May when Obleutnant Detlev Krankenhagen's *U-549* put three torpedoes into the CVE, although she was the only US carrier sunk in the entire Atlantic campaign. VC-55 lost all eight of its TBM-1Cs and three TBF-1s.

In all, US Navy escort carrier aircraft sank nine submarines in the Atlantic during 1944. The last of these was on 20 August when several VC-69 TBMs off *Bogue* sank *U-1229*. Thus, *Bogue's* aircraft had put under the first and last U-boat sunk by American hunter-killer aircraft. Although 1944 sinkings were considerably fewer than the year before, things were even rougher for the submarines. Previously, they had been free from air attack at night, and a nocturnal surface engagement was a favourite U-boat technique. But no more.

The first CVE night operations were inaugurated by *Card* in February 1944. Two TBFs had been modified for the 'Night Owl' role. They were stripped of all unessential equipment and personnel – guns, ordnance and armour plate were removed to allow installation of extra fuel tanks which, if necessary, could give an Avenger a 14-hour endurance. The pilot was accompanied only by a radar operator. At dusk on 13 February, the two Avengers were launched, and patrolled 80 miles to either side of the convoy. Without weapons, they had no means to attack a submarine, but they were intended solely to direct destroyers to the contact. Although no U-boats were found during this brief experiment, it led the way to less impromptu measures.

VC-58, under Cdr Richard Gould, went aboard *Guadalcanal* at Norfolk, Virginia, during March. The captain was Daniel V Gallery, a popular officer who believed CVEs could fly their aircraft round the clock. Both Gould and the landing signal officer agreed to try Gallery's idea for full-time night flying, and the unit trained accordingly.

The plan was to keep four armed Avengers in the air during the night. Since they were not modified to carry extra fuel, they were comfortably limited to four hours on each patrol, and would therefore require relief. This meant *Guadalcanal* would operate eight Avengers in two relays each night. After the pilots had qualified for night landings, rough weather was the only factor posing a serious threat to the plan.

VC-58 began its night patrols on 7 April, hunting south of the Azores. The first night brought no contacts, but on the night of the eighth an Avenger surprised *U-515* recharging her batteries on the surface. The TBM delivered a depth bomb attack which forced the boat down only 30 miles from the carrier. Other Avengers were delegated to remain on the scene while three destroyers sped to the contact point.

Twice during the night, the U-boat came up, but was forced down as soon as it broke surface. Throughout the following day destroyers tracked the sub, delivering depth charge attacks. Heavily damaged, *U-515* finally surfaced within gun range of the escorts and surrendered.

The VC-58 Avengers did not have to share the next kill. A hundred miles to the south-east, another sub was tracked down by the night-flying TBMs and was caught at dawn, running east. Two Avengers and a Wildcat came out of the darkness to the west, their target silhouetted against the sunrise. U-68 attempted to crash dive but it was too late. She was blown in two by a combination of depth bombs and rockets.

As 'Cap'n Dan' Gallery said, 'This settled all doubt about night operations. In a month of constant daylight flying, we had seen no subs. In 48 hours of night operations, we had two kills.'

The 30 U-boats sunk by American CVE aircraft and two shared kills with destroyers during 1943-44 were a very small portion of the total 780 sent to the bottom during the entire war. But the Battle of the Atlantic had so dramatically reversed course by 1945 that no sinkings were made by Avengers or Wildcats in the five months before VE-Day. The day-to-day impact of the escort carrier squadrons – their mere presence – was almost beyond computation. How many submarine attacks were spoiled or prevented can never be fully known.

Despite their undoubted success against the wolfpacks, Avengers and other ASW aircraft sustained casualties. Throughout the war the U-boats' heavy armament resulted in some 110 Allied aircraft being shot down, including at least five US Avengers and two Wildcats from June 1943 to September 1944. In direct exchange for these losses, three submarines were sunk. *U-262* and *U-860* each shot down two American aircraft, although the latter boat was lost in the process.

This *Block Island* crew participated in the first US rocket attack on an enemy submarine after the pilot, Lt(jg) Leonard L McFord (centre), sighted the U-boat on the surface. His crewmen were ARM3/c Charles M Gertsch (left) and AMM2/c W H Ryder (right). Also engaged in the attack was the crew of Lt(jg) Willis Seeley (*Grumman*)

Two days before D-Day, the US Navy achieved a major coup in the Battle of the Atlantic. Rear Adm Daniel Gallery's *Guadalcanal* task group forced U-505 to surface near the Azores, where the submarine crew abandoned ship, expecting the boat to sink. However, Gallery's well-prepared team boarded the sub and captured her intact, along with invaluable intelligence data. A TBF flies over U-505 which, at this point, was still in danger of foundering (*Grumman*)

TORCH AND LEADER

Three TBF squadrons supported Operation *Torch*, the American invasion of French Morocco in November 1942. Flying from escort carriers were VGS-26 aboard *Sangamon* (9 TBF-1s and 9 SBD-3s), VGS-27 in *Suwannee* (9 TBF-1s) and VGS-29 aboard *Santee* (9 TBF-1s and 9 SBD-3s). The other US carrier involved, *Ranger* (CV 4), operated an SBD and two F4F units, but no TBFs.

On the first day of *Torch* (8 November) a *Sangamon* Avenger attacking Port Lyuatey airfield was intercepted by a Dewoitine D.520. The TBF pilot, Lt R M Jones, turned into the threat and briefly exchanged gunfire with the Vichy fighter. Returning to his assigned mission, Jones bombed a flak battery, which in turn inflicted heavy damage on his TBF. He found he was unable to lower his landing flaps, but still managed a safe landing aboard *Sangamon*. Later that day, two VGS-29 Avengers crashed on launch from *Santee*, but both crews were rescued.

The next day a *Santee* TBF was hit by flak and force landed near Bou Guedra. The wounded pilot, Lt(jg) Charles Rodeen, was captured with his gunner. On the 10th a VGS-27 crew was killed while landing aboard *Suwannee*. Ens Robert O'Neil had an 'in-flight engagement' when his tailhook grabbed an arresting wire before the wheels touched the deck. The TBF was pitched overboard, and its depth charges exploded on impact, killing the three-man crew.

The 27 TBFs sustained 10 losses to all causes, very few of which were combat related. In fact, the 37 per cent loss rate was the highest for any navy aircraft engaged in *Torch*, ans was mainly attributed to the relative inexperience of the escort scouting pilots. Heaviest casualties were sustained by *Santee*, which wrote off seven of nine Avengers.

Despite the losses, there were occasional successes, as three VGS-27 Avengers off *Suwannee* claimed a French submarine to score the first kill for CVE aircraft. However, U-boats were aggressively active, and on the 11th and 12th alone, they sank four transports, damaged two other ships, and fired torpedoes at three carriers and a cruiser.

OPERATION *LEADER*

US Navy TBFs conducted one operation above the Arctic Circle in World War 2 – Operation *Leader*, a strike against Axis-controlled shipping in October 1943. Sailing alongside the British Home Fleet, USS *Ranger* embarked Air Group 4 to attack Bodø harbour, in Norway.

Located on the Saltfjord, Bodø was targeted on 4 October with two strikes. The first, composed of 20 SBD-5s and 8 F4F-4s, launched shortly after 0700. The second launch included ten Avengers of VT-4, escorted by half a dozen Wildcats. One TBF was downed by German flak while ingressing to the target, but the other Grummans sank a freighter previously damaged by the Dauntlesses.

PACIFIC PREDATORS

In the Pacific, 1945 was by far the most active year for Avenger sub hunters. The only previous period of much activity had occurred during November 1943 and the invasion of the Gilbert Islands. *Chenango* aircraft had sunk I-21 on the 29th, but as in the Atlantic, an enemy sub had picked off a CVE – *Liscombe Bay* sunk in 23 minutes

Despite the efficacy of the U-boat 'fight back' doctrine that accounted for at least seven American carrier aircraft, greater perils lay in conducting ordinary flight operations. This *Bogue* Avenger (unlucky number 13) broke an arresting wire, nearly struck a deck hand, and plunged into the island with predictable results for the airframe (*National Archives*)

after being hit by torpedoes from I-175 on 24 November. Unlike the fortunate crew of *Block Island*, *Liscombe Bay* suffered heavy loss of life.

Only two sub kills were made by Avengers in the Pacific during 1944. The first occurred on 19 June, at the height of the Battle of the Philippine Sea, when Ens G E Sabin of VT-60 off *Suwannee* sent I-184 into a final dive near Guam in the Marianas. Five months later, on 18 November, *Anzio* aircraft teamed up with a destroyer escort to end the career of I-41 some 300 miles east of Samar.

Anzio was to the Pacific CVEs what *Bogue* was to those in the Atlantic: the first and last hunter-killer to sink an enemy sub, and the most successful to boot. During the bloody battle for Iwo Jima, *Anzio's* VC-13 sank two submarines on consecutive days: an RO boat of 960 tons on 26 February 1945 and a big I-boat on the 27th.

VC-92 off *Tulagi* finished an I-boat at the end of April during the Okinawa campaign, and then *Anzio* scored again a month later, sinking *I-361* unassisted. *Anzio's* last victim was unlucky *I-13*, destroyed in collaboration with a destroyer escort on 16 July, some 550 miles east of Yokosuka. Of the six fleet submarines credited to CVEs in the Pacific, *Anzio* accounted for three by herself, plus both of the shared kills. The sinking of Japanese midget submarines is difficult to document.

To round out the story, we must return to the Atlantic in June 1944, only five months after *Suwannee* aircraft had sunk *I-184* off Guam. *I-52* was on a special liaison mission to France, and was first located by a night-flying *Bogue* Avenger south-west of the Azores on 23 June. Lt Cdr Jesse Taylor, VC-69's CO, subsequently picked up the radar contact and dropped a flare, which illuminated the 350-ft monster, drove it down with a bombing attack, and dropped a sonobuoy. Although the Japanese skipper evaded Taylor, he survived only a few hours. Shortly before 0100 on the 24th, another *Bogue* TBF followed sonobuoy contacts and executed a depth-bomb attack in the darkness. After dawn a destroyer patrolling the area picked up a Japanese sandal and five dozen bales of crude rubber floating among the debris.

The final tally for submarine sinkings by US Navy CVE aircraft was 31 in the Atlantic (including one Vichy French and one Japanese) and six in the Pacific, plus two German and two Japanese boats shared with escort vessels. The campaign which the Avenger waged in the Atlantic was probably as typical of war itself as any aspect of World War 2. Mostly it was hours and days and weeks of dull routine – of monotonous, uneventful patrols during which nothing was seen and almost nothing happened.

Then there were the few times when a contact actually developed into an attack. And then there was too much to do in the time available. The sub had to be reported with an accurate position fix, and additional aircraft summoned. The attack had to be co-ordinated and delivered, often in the face of

Rear Adm Reed and Capt Vosseler pose with the trophies of the hunt: *Bogue's* scoreboard showing 12 Axis submarines sunk by the ship's task group as of October 1944. Nine of the kills were credited to the five composite squadrons assigned to *Bogue* during that period. (*National Archives*)

A fish hook was an inspired choice for the emblem of an anti-submarine aircraft. This VC-97 TBM-3, based aboard the escort carrier *Makassar Strait*, patrols near Okinawa. Although neither the ship nor squadron claimed a kill, other Pacific Fleet CVEs succeeded in destroying at least six Japanese boats (*Author's collection*)

The Avenger's first anti-submarine success came during Operation *Torch* when a *Suwannee* aircraft sank a Vichy French boat in November 1942. This VGS-26 TBF was photographed conducting carrier qualifications aboard *Charger* in July 1942 (*Author's collection*)

formidable AA fire. There was the constant gnawing anxiety that this opportunity – the one thing for which the pilot and crew had trained for months and might never come again – could go wrong. And sometimes it did. The aim was hurried or misjudged. The sub dived while still out of range. Or the aircraft fell to well-directed automatic weapons fire.

But now and then, just often enough to keep up morale, a tangible result was obtained in the form of a definite kill. Oil slick and debris bubbling to the surface, the sight of U-boat men bobbing in the water, or even the spectacle of a sub breaking in two and plunging out of sight. These were the dramatic consequences of a successful attack.

However, they were not the most important result. They were not the end, but the means to an end. The unheralded, but war-winning, result was a convoy arriving at its destination with few or no losses.

It would be unfair and inaccurate to say the Avenger was responsible for winning the Battle of the Atlantic. But there can be no doubt that it was the dominant aircraft engaged in that six-year struggle – the only aspect of the war that Winston Churchill feared the Allies might lose. Because of the importance of keeping open the sea lanes between the 'Old World' and the 'New', the Avenger's part in defeating the U-boats must be considered its most significant contribution to victory.

Submarine kills by CVE Squadrons

Atlantic 1942-45

VC-9	*Bogue, Card*	9
VC-13	*Core, Guadalcanal*	6
VC-1	*Card, Block Island*	5
VC-29	*Santee*	3
VC-58	*Guadalcanal, Wake Island*	3 (1 shared)
VC-6	*Block Island*	2 (1 shared)
VGS-27	*Suwannee*	1 (Vichy French)
VC-42	*Bogue*	1
VC-65	*Bogue*	1 (Japanese boat)
VC-95	*Bogue*	1 (shared)

Pacific 1944-45 (excludes Midget Submarines)

VC-82	*Anzio*	3 (1 shared)
VC-13	*Anzio*	2 (1 shared)
VT-60	*Suwannee*	1
VC-92	*Tulagi*	1

ROYAL NAVY AND RNZAF

ritain received nearly 1000 TBFs and TBMs – 402 TBF-1Bs as Avenger Is, 334 TBM-1Cs as Avenger IIs and 222 TBM-3s as Mk IIIs. Seventeen frontline FAA squadrons flew Avengers during the war, with 20 others providing training or logistics support at home and abroad. Additionally, two Royal New Zealand Air Force squadrons flew TBFs in the Southwest Pacific.

The Royal Navy received its first 15 TBF-1s before the end of 1942. Suffering an acute shortage of modern carrier-based strike aircraft, the Fleet Air Arm quickly took to the Avenger. But until January 1944, the TBF was known as the Tarpon in British service, after the large warm water fish of the Western Atlantic.

Whether Tarpon or Avenger, the big Grumman was badly needed by the Commonwealth services. The ageing, but tireless, Fairey Swordfish remained in service until the end of the war, but the 'Stringbag' biplane design, with its limited speed, clearly marked it as obsolete. Of questionable value was Fairey's follow-on, the ungainly looking Barracuda torpedo/dive-bomber. The Barracuda suffered a six-year gestation period, and by the time it became available in any

Pilots and aircrew of No 849 Sqn, Fleet Air Arm, at NAS Squantum, Massachusetts, in August 1943. The original complement was 12 aircraft, which was eventually reduced to nine so as to make room aboard escort carriers for Martlet/Wildcat fighters. The squadron deployed in HMS *Khedive*, *Rajah*, and *Victorious*. Of note is the variety of American and British flying equipment – life preservers, parachute harnesses and helmets (*Grumman*)

numbers, it was well past its prime. Recalled one veteran FAA pilot, 'The Barracuda was a good dive-bomber. Every time you reduced power, it went into a dive'. By October 1944 Avengers had replaced Barracudas aboard the British Pacific Fleet carriers.

Yet another Fairey strike aircraft, the versatile Firefly, arrived late in the war. It was a modern, useful machine, heavily armed with good range. However, as a two-seater it was neither a fighter nor a bomber. It was, perhaps, the first purely naval strike aircraft.

The first FAA Avenger squadron was No 832, previously equipped with Fairey Albacores. The squadron received 15 TBF-1s at NAS Norfolk, Virginia, in January 1943 during the refit of HMS *Victorious*. The squadron exchanged its Albacore biplanes for Tarpons on New Year's Day 1943, and by that spring, *Victorious* was in the South Pacific training with USS *Saratoga*. The TBFs of No 832 flew from *Victorious* with three FAA Martlet fighter units on missions over the Solomon Islands in June and July 1943. Their objective was to prevent the Japanese Navy from interfering with the invasion of the New Georgia group, but as the enemy fleet failed to contest the landings, little happened. *Victorious* returned to Britain, leaving some of her TBFs with *Saratoga*.

The first actual Tarpon squadron was No 845, which received its Grummans at NAS Quonset Point in April 1943. Following at two-month intervals were Nos 848 and 849 Sqns, and with accelerating production, eight other FAA units (Nos 850-857) stood up at NAAS Squantum, Massachusetts, from September 1943 to April 1944.

Originally, Tarpons were expected to fly with four-man crews:

This Tarpon I of No 846 Sqn was photographed by the legendary Charles E Brown during a press day organised by the Fleet Air Arm at Macrihanish, in Scotland, in December 1943. The event was staged so as to introduce the new type to the British public (*Charles E Brown via Philip Jarrett*)

An anonymous Tarpon I overflies a convoy, and its escort carrier, at the end of a long ASW patrol. Note the bulged fuselage window forward of the roundel, this fitment being peculiar to British Avengers. It improved visibility, as observers originally rode in the radioman's compartment (*via Philip Jarrett*)

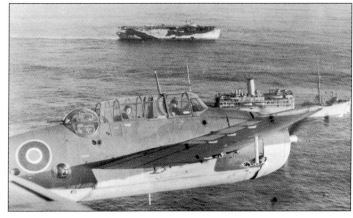

Framed by the float of an amphibian, Avenger Is warm up their engines on the flightline of a naval air station. Grumman built these aircraft to Fleet Air Arm specifications, and painted them on the production line alongside those Avengers destined for the US Navy and Marine Corps (*Grumman*)

pilot, bombardier/turret gunner, radioman (telegraphist) and observer. However, the tunnel position was too small to accommodate both the radioman and observer, and eventually most FAA squadrons seem to have adopted the usual American three-man crew.

AGAINST THE WOLFPACKS

Like their US counterparts, FAA Avengers hunted U-boats. But they were engaged on a far smaller scale, as the venerable Swordfish was much more numerous aboard British CVEs in European waters. From 1940 to 1945, FAA aircraft sank 18 Axis submarines and shared in 16 other sinkings with escort vessels or RAF units. The biplane Swordfish accounted for 15 of the solo kills and participated in another 10.

However, the Avenger was the next most successful FAA sub hunter. Four U-boats succumbed in whole or in part to Royal Navy TBMs. No 846 Sqn was the premier anti-U-boat Avenger unit, being credited with one whole kill, one shared and two assists.

The squadron's first two successes came within three days of one another in early April 1944. Escorting Arctic convoy RA-58, No 846 Sqn was embarked aboard HMS *Tracker* while Swordfish of No 819 Sqn flew from *Activity*. The two units hunted aggressively, and on the first of the month No 846 Avengers helped HMS *Beagle* sniff out and run to bay *U-355*. Two days later No 819's Swordfish joined *Tracker* Avengers in finishing off *U-288*.

The Avenger's only sub kill in the Indian Ocean was very much a team effort. TBMs from No 832 Sqn aboard HMS *Begum* and No 851 Sqn in *Shah* destroyed U-198 on 12 August 1944 in concert with British and Indian frigates.

There were no more anti-sub successes for FAA Avengers until the last month of the European war. On 4 May 1945 three Royal Navy CVEs launched 44 Avengers and Wildcats against German shipping at Kilbotn, in Norway. No 846 Sqn, now embarked in HMS *Trumpeter*, did most of the damage. Her Avengers sank a moored depot ship and *U-711*, which was secured alongside. HMS *Queen's* No 853 Sqn sank another ship in the same attack, the last made by the Fleet Air Arm in Europe. One Avenger and one Wildcat were shot down by flak. Three days later Germany surrendered.

Avenger JZ300 was badly shot up during a glide bombing attack on German shipping at St Malo, France, on the Brittany coast, during June 1944. Sub-Lt Thomas Derrick-White of No 855 Sqn was one of six FAA pilots on the mission, and his aircraft was struck by light and medium flak during the low-level pullout. Ordering his crew to prepare for a water landing, and although wounded in the back, Derrick-White found that his aircraft was controllable, and he managed a fast landing at a coastal emergency strip, despite poor weather and loss of his port stabiliser and elevator. Only then did the pilot learn that the observer riding behind him was dead. Additionally, the starboard stabiliser had a five-inch hole, and the canopy was shattered, with 36 holes (*Grumman*)

The empennage of JZ300, showing the port stabiliser severed almost at the fuselage. The outboard former is badly bent and a control rod severed (*Grumman*)

In addition to the anti-submarine role, FAA Avengers flew numerous other missions against German forces. Perhaps the least known was support of the D-Day landings by Royal Navy squadrons based in south-eastern England. These included No 155 Wing at Manston, which included No 848 Sqn, teamed with RAF Beaufighters. At Hawkinge No 157 Wing comprised Nos 854 and 855 Sqns. Patrolling the South-western Approaches from Perranparth was No 156 Wing with Nos 849 and 850 Sqns.

During the last 12 months of the European war, CVE aircraft logged some 30 attacks against facilities and shipping in Norway, frequently with mines. By far the most common opposition was German flak, but HMS *Trumpeter* lost a No 846 Sqn aircraft to Luftwaffe fighters in August 1944. That month British Avengers also participated in the third of a series of strikes against the German battleship *Tirpitz*, anchored in a Norwegian fjord.

AGAINST THE RISING SUN

Undoubtedly the most successful operation involving Royal Navy Avengers was the two-phase strike on Sumatran oil fields in January 1945. Operation *Meridian* involved four carriers: *Indomitable* with No 857 Sqn; *Illustrious* with No 854; *Victorious* with No 849; and *Indefatigable* with No 820.

These squadrons totalled 65 Avengers, supported by some 170 Hellcats, Corsairs, Seafires and Fireflies.

The first strike was launched against facilities at Pladjoe by 47 Avengers, all armed with four 500-lb bombs, on 24 January. Another

This catapult shot from HMS *Trumpeter* catches an Avenger just lifting off the deck. The 'booster' is at full stroke, with the bridle slung forward between the aircraft's wheels. Most Avenger launches from escort carrier required the catapult to generate sufficient speed, as the ships were seldom capable of more than 18 knots. (*Author's collection*)

Boosters are mighty fine things! *Ameer* conducts 'flanchor' operations (flying at anchor) in Trincomalee Harbour, Ceylon, by catapulting a No 845 Sqn aircraft while moored alongside a replenishment ship (*Author's collection*)

Fleet Air Arm Avengers flew several strikes in Scandinavian waters against German and other Axis-controlled shipping. This shot depicts the approach to Svino Fjord, on the rocky Norwegian coast, in 1944 (*Author's collection*)

An Avenger III takes a 'wave around' after overshooting the flightdeck, and will make another circuit. The British Pacific Fleet adopted US style horizontal bars to the blue and white cockade in 1945 as further insurance against confusing friendly with enemy aircraft insignia (*via Philip Jarrett*)

flight of four attacked Japanese airfields in the area. Hellcats and Corsairs provided fighter escort.

Things did not go well with the TBMs in the beginning. Seven Avengers were forced to abort or were damaged in flightdeck accidents. But surprise was achieved, as no fighter interception was made until after the target had been hit. In fact, no flak was encountered until the TBMs were in their dives. The bombing was accurate, with considerable damage inflicted upon the refinery.

There was surprise for the aircrews, though. During their dive to bombing altitude they were astonished to see barrage balloons suddenly in their midst. No aircraft struck these obstacles, but they boded no good for the future. Two Avengers, one each from *Indomitable* and *Indefatigable*, failed to return – the 'Indomit' aircraft was shot down by a Japanese fighter.

In all, the carrier had lost nine aircraft, but an estimated 30 per cent of Pladjoe's facilities had been destroyed.

Five days later the task force returned to Sumatran waters on the 29th, dealing with Soengi Gerong. The strike group was nearly identical to that of the 24th, with Lt Cdr W J Mainprice, CO of *Illustrious'* No 854 Sqn, as bomber leader. He was informed that any balloons protecting the target would be destroyed before his formation arrived.

The strike was launched early in the morning under low ceiling and reduced visibility. One Avenger lost power and splashed into a water landing while three more aborted with engine trouble.

This time there was no surprise. Japanese fighters were up and waiting, the AA guns were alerted, and most of the balloons remained aloft. Despite this formidable defence, the TBMs pressed their attacks with determination and accuracy. However, Lt Cdr Mainprice hit a balloon cable during his dive on the target and was killed with his crew. His wingman's plane also snagged a cable, again with loss of all aboard.

Departing the burning oil tanks and bombed facilities, the Avengers headed for the rendezvous in singles and small formations. At this point they were vulnerable to interception, and No 849 lost two aeroplanes to defending JAAF fighters. But the Avengers could defend themselves, too. A pair of No 820 Squadron pilots off *Indefatigable* fought a Nakajima Ki-44, which expended its ammunition in numerous passes, then pulled up ahead of Sub-Lt W Coster, who fired all his .50-cal load at the 'Tojo'. The Nakajima fighter was last seen dropping toward the trees, streaming smoke and flames.

Lt G J Connolly of No 854 Sqn spotted two 'Tojos' harrying a No 849 Sqn TBM low over the tree-tops. Diving to the attack, he shot down one and, drawing the attention of the other, was able to disengage and escort the damaged *Victorious* bomber to the task force. Numerous Avengers were shot up from flak and fighters – the crews

complained about lack of adequate escort – and six ditched near the fleet. Fortunately, these crews were rescued, but 19 pilots or aircrew were lost with 11 Avengers shot down or force-landed.

Despite heavy losses, the Grummans were mainly responsible for cutting Sumatra's aviation fuel production by two-thirds at a time when Japan could least afford it.

The British Pacific Fleet TBMs continued their work at Okinawa, Formosa and over Japan itself for the remainder of the year. At war's end the Fleet Air Arm had seven deployed Avenger squadrons: Nos 845 and 851's Avenger Is in HMS *Shah*, operating in the East Indies; and with the British Pacific Fleet were No 820's Mk Is aboard *Indefatigable*; No 828 (Mks I and II) in *Implacable*; No 848 (Mks I and II) in *Formidable*; No 849 (Mks I and II) in *Victorious*; and No 857 (Mks I and II) aboard *Indomitable*.

Subsequently, 170 dedicated ASW Avenger IVs (AS Mk 4) went to the Fleet Air Arm after the war. Thus the Avenger proved a success in two navies in both hemispheres. Few aircraft can claim a similar record.

KIWI AVENGERS

The Royal New Zealand Air Force flew a variety of Allied aircraft during World War 2, including naval types such as the Douglas SBD Dauntless and Vought F4U Corsair. Forty-eight TBF-1s and -1Cs were provided to the Kiwis in mid-1943 and assigned to No 30 and 31 Sqns, which carried the dive-bomber designation. Formed between September and December of that year, the two units each logged a 1944 combat tour under the control of Solomons Strike Command before being stood down.

At war's end nine of the RNZAF Avengers went to the Royal Navy and 16 were returned to their original 'owner'. The balance of the surviving airframes enjoyed a lengthy if unglamorous career in New Zealand service for the next 15 years. The last two Kiwi TBFs were withdrawn in 1960.

New Zealand's first Avenger squadron was No 30, formed in September 1943. This TBF-1C (NZ2510) was based at Turtle Bay airstrip on Espiritu Santo, in the New Hebrides, during March 1944. It bears standard RNZAF markings over the usual American tri-colour scheme. The second 'Kiwi' squadron, No 31, also logged a Solomon Islands tour before both units were disbanded in 1944 (*Author's collection*)

TBF-1 NZ2544 was written off following combat damage over Bougainville on 28 May 1944 (*via Bruce Robertson*)

ASSESSMENT

The Avenger was one of the three most numerous carrier aircraft of all time, and the most-produced attack type. With 2293 TBFs and 7546 TBMs, the total production of 9839 Avengers was exceeded only by 12,570 Corsairs and 12,275 Hellcats. The Grumman/Eastern collaboration also produced the fourth-ranked 'tail-hook' aircraft with 7905 F4F/FM Wildcats built between 1940-45.

Avengers continued on active service in the US Navy until 1954, when they were retired from the anti-submarine and carrier onboard delivery (COD) roles. TBMs also flew with Britain and other allied navies after 1945, including the Japanese Maritime Self-Defense Force.

However, the TBF/TBM's role on the world stage occurred wholly between June 1942 and August 1945. Those 38 months took Avenger squadrons from the sweltering tropic heat of the Solomon Islands to frigid arctic temperatures of the Scandinavian coast. Aviators of four services flew the type in combat, including the United States Navy and Marine Corps, the Royal Navy and the Royal New Zealand Air Force. They employed weapons as diverse as bombs, torpedoes, rockets and mines to sink Japanese battleships and carriers, German submarines and Axis-controlled Norwegian freighters.

FLYING THE AVENGER

Lt Henry A Suerstedt was a pilot in VC-21 from October 1943 until July 1945, flying from the escort carriers *Marcus Island* and *Commencement Bay*. His combat experience reached from the Palau Islands through the Philippine campaign, and included sinking a Japanese midget submarine;

'The TBF/TBM was very heavy on the controls. It was flown by constant use of the elevator trim tab since the longitudinal aerodynamic forces were extremely difficult to physically overcome without the tab. I know other old TBF pilots who disagree with this assessment, however.

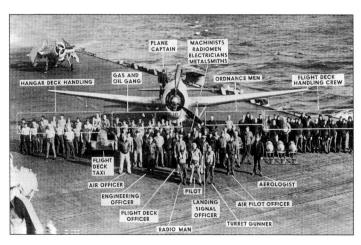

This 1943 photo depicts the team effort required to put an Avenger crew in the air for a combat mission. There are 24 flightdeck and 19 hangar deck crewmen; a dozen men to handle and dispense aviation fuel and oil; 23 engine, airfram, and radio mechanics, including the plane captain; seven ordnancemen; and six air staff officers for meteorology, planning and flightdeck control, and the landing signal officer. A total of 91 men to put the TBF's three-man crew over a target! (*Grumman*)

'I recall routinely using the inside of both my knees to control the lateral wing position of the aircraft. It was not normally desirable to change the aileron trim tabs since any change in the control force required was usually of a transient nature. Using leg force on the stick for lateral control worked quite satisfactorily.

'My primary concern was that if one did not lead the lowering of landing flags with great forward throws of the trim tab wheel, the change in trim could send the plane into a significant nose-up attitude.

'Carrier landings were not too difficult in TBFs or TBMs. After the "cut" by the LSO, and dropping the aircraft's nose, I always utilised my right hand and left wrist to pull the stick back forcefully in order to get the tail down for the wire engagement. Because the *Casablanca* class CVE (as I recall) had only six or seven arresting wires, and perhaps only five before barrier engagement, "diving for the deck" was not frowned upon if it was done reasonably well. The pilots always considered it an easy out for the LSO to claim that this was the cause of an accident, and not the LSO's signals! What it did cause was an inordinate amount of TBF/TBM type "blowouts". If a pilot consistently tried for the number two wire, as I did, the TBM landed on the after elevator, which tilted the elevator forward and resulted in as much as a four to five-inch "curb" for the aircraft wheels to hit. There seemed to be far less recrimination and retribution for several blown tyres as compared to one barrier engagement!

'Aerodynamically, the TBM was an extremely predictable and honest aircraft, although somewhat cumbersome. When coming aboard in bad weather on a pitching deck, on a few occasions when slow and high at the "cut", once the nose dropped through, the aircraft required a momentary burst of full power in order to get the tail down. This kept the aircraft from dropping to the deck nose-down on the main landing gear, but it was most stimulating to roll to a stop, arrested by number two or three wire, and hear the air officer's "crash yodeller" still warbling and find yourself surrounded by crash and rescue teams.

'The Wright R-2600 engine left something to be desired, and sometimes it delivered barely enough power after take-off to stay marginally airborne. This involved the routine heavy launch from a CVE, or an occasional incident such as pulling an unreleasable gunnery banner through the main portion of Kennewick, Washington, *and* their north-south phone lines. However, reliability on long flights seemed good.

'There were such instances as rolling into a dive of 14,000 ft with the prop in low pitch (as a brake in the dive) and high blower because of the altitude, and pulling out low on a high-speed recovery after massive enemy opposition, only to discover in great dismay that the engine was still at full throttle, low pitch (i.e., high prop RPM) with an astronomical amount of manifold pressure – like 57 inches of mercury! The fact that the R-2600 held together and functioned after that had to be a tribute to the engine design, and the people responsible for it.

'Our aircrewmen were, as a whole, outstanding. No doubt in World War 2 there was a small percentage who should have been doing something else, but the aircrew did all they were trained to do, and a lot more. The radioman who flew with me in VC-21 was even checked out in the remote-control system originally intended as part of the

Right
A practice torpedo attack is flown by early-production TBFs. The leading Avengers have already broken away following their drops, and the next aeroplane in line has released its torpedo. Depending on estimated speed and range of the target vessel, wingmen would add or detract five-knot increments in an attempt to bracket the ship with a 'comb' of torpedoes that would ensure at least one hit from either beam. Properly executed, a squadron-sized attack could be completed in less than one minute from the run-in point to typical drop distance of 800 yards. Barely 20 seconds later, one or more torpedoes should strike the target. When the TBF first entered service in 1942, the torpedo was the limiting factor in its combat operations. Originally, the Mk XIII weapon had to be released from little more than 50 ft, and no more than 110 knots, which posed a difficult tactical problem for 'TorpRons'. Later modifications permitted higher release altitudes, but the US Navy fought the first 18 months of the Pacific War with substandard torpedoes (*Grumman*)

Lt Henry A Suerstedt, Avenger pilot of VC-21, embarked in the escort carriers *Marcus Island* and *Commencement Bay* during 1944-45. Apart from routine missions during the Seventh Fleet's sweep through the Central Pacific, Suerstedt was credited with sinking a Japanese midget submarine in the Philippines, and subsequently commanded TBM squadron VA-213 shortly before the Korean War (*Author's collection*)

Norden bombsight. He had only lateral control through the Pilot Position Indicator, but we practised to the point where we could engage it as we came off the target, after regaining level flight, and the radioman could find his way more or less back to the task group.

'I always insisted on a turret gunner who was also an aircraft mechanic. He not only could reassure me when the engine would go into "automatic rough" at the 250-mile turn in a long search, but could also utilise his talents in other situations. Because of battle damage to the throttle linkage, I had to land at the marginally US-held airstrip on Peleliu. The only aircraft in there prior to mine was an SB2C, which had spun in a day or so before trying to land with severe damage. My gunner used his mechanical training to advantage by rapidly cannibalising the requisite parts from a wrecked Mitsubishi 'Betty', and thus saved the day for us. We returned to the ship in good shape, being chased off Peleliu by a Japanese mortar!'

Suerstedt continued flying the TBM after the war, ending his association with the Avenger as CO of VA-213. 'Hank' Suerstedt died in Coronado, California, in 1990.

'THE CHEAP SEATS'

The Avenger's radio compartment, well aft in the fuselage, was not for the claustrophobic. However, some vital mission functions were

Every bombing mission begins with the 'ordies' – ordnancemen who load and arm the weapons. The sailor on the left winds a moveable winch to raise the '250-pounder' into the bomb bay, where it will be affixed to shackles, while the man on the right wears a 'key chain' about his neck with safety wires that will be removed from the nose and tail fuses when the bombs are made 'hot'. This photo also provides an excellent look at the TBF's double-hinged bomb bay doors (*Grumman*)

performed there, including radar search and track, as well as defence of the aircraft from enemy fighter attack in the vulnerable six o'clock low position. One flier who logged many hours in 'the cheap seats' (so named for the poor view) was Lt William B Chace, who helped inaugurate airborne radar to carrier aviation;

'The TBF offered its crew great rewards, and some vexations, which is, I guess, the prerogative of a big, beautiful babe – and that she was.

'The tunnel position did not provide much comfort. It was a noisy, enclosed, capsule with very limited visibility. After days of intensive combat, it became encrusted with, and smelled of, engine oil and hydraulic fluids. There was no physical access to the cockpit, therefore it could produce a discouraging claustrophobia for the uninitiated.

'In the summer of 1942 a radioman in Torpedo Squadron Six died of carbon monoxide poisoning while in the landing circle waiting to board the *Saratoga*. This tragedy shook us all, and generally caused pandemonium until it was determined that he had vented a small port in the tail designed to eject spent .30-cal shell cases. Unfortunately, exhaust fumes had been sucked into the tunnel rather than fresh air. When exhaustive investigation determined the cause, AlNav advices were circulated, and I know of no other tragic instances.

'As I can personally attest, the spaciousness and configuration of the tunnel mandated that loose gear be well secured during take-off and landing. On the squally, black night of 25 January 1944, TF-58 was making a fast run in to support initial landings at Kwajalein. Among the force was *Enterprise*, whose mission was to launch a pre-dawn fighter sweep to interdict the airbase on Maloelap Atoll.

'As zero hour approached, it became apparent that with almost no visibility, launch would be difficult and rendezvous of the Hellcats nearly impossible. Therefore, it was decided that Cdr Roscoe Newman would be launched first in a radar-equipped TBF to serve as a reference point for the F6Fs. I would be observer at my radar in the tunnel.

'It was a catapult launch. Since radar was the name of the game that night, electronics technicians were swarming about the plane until we were locked onto the catapult. The engine revved, the launch signal flashed. Sometime later I heard a distant voice in my earphones. "Pilot to radar, where are you?" After a few repeats, I came to and responded. One of the technicians had left a black box loose atop the radar, and it had socked me right between the eyes on launch. Under nearly impossible visibility conditions, Cdr Newman assisted a partial rendezvous and vector for 15 or so Hellcats. Taroa ceased to be a threat, and Kwajalein is history. Back on deck, he questioned my early lack of response. I could think of no better reply than a diffident, "A little electronic trouble, sir".'

Reservist Lt William B Chace was a qualified naval aviation observer who flew 'the cheap seats' in VT-10 Avengers from *Enterprise* during 1943-44. His speciality was airborne radar, both detecting suitable surface targets and providing navigation aid to other 'Big E' aircraft during pre-dawn launches and join-ups (*Chace*)

TURRET VIEW

Charles M Westbrook joined the navy in 1942 and, following aviation mechanic school and gunnery training, he was assigned to VC-10 in 1943. As an aviation machinist mate second class, he flew from the escort carrier *Gambier Bay* in the Marianas, Palaus and Philippines campaigns. He remained with the ship until she was sunk off Samar during the Battle of Leyte Gulf in October 1944;

'From gunnery school I was sent to flight school in Florida. There, we were assigned to crews of three: pilot, radioman and gunner. We learned to check the plane before flights for full gas tanks, oil, tyres, controls and sometimes to even start the engine for a ground test. Also, the guns were inspected and ammunition loaded. This included the gunner's turret .50-cal and the pilot's wing guns. The radioman took care of his radio and radar, along with his .30-cal.

'The training in Florida was torpedo runs with dummy warheads, dive and skip-bombing, and gunnery flights. Another function was patrol. We carried live loads on these flights over the Atlantic, as U-boats were still found occasionally.

'In November 1943 I went to Seattle, Washington, to join VC-10. The skipper was Lt Cdr Ed Huxtable, and I still remember one of the first things he said. Mr Huxtable told us, "When you have the duty to fly, you had better be here and be sober!"

'I think it was in March 1944 that we were assigned to our regular pilots. I was with Ens Hovey Seymour, the prewar Yale football star, and Larry Austin was radioman. On our second shakedown cruise, the full crews were to fly. We went out to pick up the carrier south-west of San Clemente. Everything went fine on the approach until we were just aft of the ship and got the "cut" signal (from the LSO). At this time Mr Seymour gave it the throttle. We went past the carrier and up for 100 ft or more. About this time the plane stalled. It turned over on the port wing and fell off to the port side of the ship. We hit the water on the nose and port wing, the tail came back above the water for about ten seconds, then sank.

'I was in the turret and got out after the plane went under, though the escape hatch was jammed at first. Larry Austin escaped through the door. I believe he had both ankles sprained from bracing his feet against the radio mounts. We never saw Mr Seymour again.

'Next morning I caught a plane to North Island, San Diego, then a bus to Brown Field. There was a new pilot on the bus – Mr Seymour's replacement, Ens Robert L Crocker. I flew with him the rest of my time in VC-10. During one of our first talks, he said not to hold back, but be sure to tell him if I didn't like the way our plane performed. After all, I was three or four years older, at age 25 or 26!'

<u>TORPEDOES</u>

The Avenger's primary weapon was intended to be the aerial torpedo. However, the US Navy's ordnance scandal of 1942-43 prevented fleet TBF units from achieving their potential in the realm of torpedo attacks, and consequently far more sorties were flown with bombs. Although a lack of warship targets between late 1942 and mid-1944 was to blame, too many opportunities were lost in those 20 months. Retired Capt Frank DeLorenzo;

'I recall that in the summer of 1941 I made several torpedo test drops flying with "Red" Raborn, who later made flag rank and headed up the Polaris missile programme. We made our drops in San Diego Bay, and had plywood tail fins attached to the torpedoes. The fins would intentionally destruct on impact with the water. Their purpose was to give the torpedo a better angle of entry. Without the fins, the

Petty Officer 2nd Class Charles M Westbrook was a turret gunner in VC-10 aboard *Gambier Bay*, which was sunk by Japanese cruisers off Samar on 25 October 1944. He wears the distinctive Combat Aircrewman's silver wings with inlaid rubies denoting multiple combat actions. Westbrook finished the war as an aircrewman in a Martin PBM Mariner squadron (*Westbrook*)

entry would be too shallow and would cause the torpedo to broach. We made several drops and kept changing the size and shape of the fins until we could consistently get a good torpedo entry angle.'

Avengers participated in the destruction of six Japanese aircraft carriers, but only two were sunk wholly or largely by torpedoes. Three battleships and 14 cruisers were also sent to the bottom in whole, or in part, by TBFs and TBMs, both with bombs and torpedoes. These figures do not include another dozen major warships attacked by Avengers (in company with other aircraft) and sunk or destroyed while in Kure Harbor during July and August 1945. These 'sitting ducks' – six carriers, three battleships and three cruisers – were mostly immobile, and their destruction gives little demonstration of the Avenger's capabilities against capital ships manoeuvring in the open sea.

One of the TorpRon commanders who experienced the frustration and eventual resurgence of torpedo attack was Lt Cdr Larry French, originally a TBD pilot who briefly transitioned to F4Fs for the Midway battle. Upon return to the TorpRon community, he waged a home front battle to bring VT-13's weapons up to their potential;

'The "ring-tail" torpedo was designed and developed by the California Institute of Technology, modifying the standard Mk 13-1A aerial torpedo with a steel band about ten inches wide around the tail fins. This ring-tail stabilised the torpedo in flight and protected the steering mechanism on contact with the water. There were some internal modifications as well.

'Cal Tech tested these torpedoes by using an old log chute to launch them into a lake. Thus you can see it was most difficult to get the navy interested and to make an aerial test. But I believe that VT-13 was the first unit in the fleet which had the ring-tail. In early 1944 while USS *Franklin* was in San Diego, I was called by the captain to attend an AirPac conference regarding the flight testing of this torpedo.

'We loaded 16 VT-13 planes at North Island with the ring-tail and the *Franklin* was the target off Point Loma. The torpedoes had dummy warheads, and depth regulators were set to pass under the carrier. The 16 torpedo planes attacked the carrier from ahead, and 30 to 45 degrees on port and starboard bows, simultaneously. They were launched at 500-800 ft altitude at speeds of 240-280 knots (275-325 mph). The altitude and airspeed varied in order to gain proper entry angle into the water. All the ring-tails appeared to run hot, straight and normal, with many "hits" reported by lookouts on the *Franklin*.

'Our tests showed the ring-tails could be launched at airspeeds up to 280 knots and altitudes as high as 800 ft. The only restriction was that the plane had to be in straight and level flight at the time of release.

'However, there were only about 56 such torpedoes in the programme at that time. The *Franklin* and I wanted all these put aboard, as we were sailing to the war zone. But due to continuation of evaluation and testing, we got 48.'

Another type of torpedo had become available in 1943, the year which represented a renaissance of naval aviation ordnance. This was the acoustical Mk 24 'Fido' anti-submarine weapon, so named because it followed its target not unlike a peg dog by homing on a submerged sub's engine noise. 'Fido', and a new 500-lb depth charge, became

Lt Cdr Larry B French was commanding officer of VT-13 aboard *Franklin* in 1944. A prewar TBD pilot who briefly transitioned to F4Fs at the time of Midway, French returned to torpedo squadrons in 1942. He was closely involved in development of the 'ring tail' modification which permitted Mk XIII torpedoes to be dropped safely from higher altitudes and at greater airspeeds (*French*)

instrumental in the Atlantic U-boat campaign during 1943, and that year accounted for nearly two dozen sinkings between them. Like conventional bombs, the depth charge could be released in singles, pairs, or salvos, depending on the pattern desired.

OTHER WEAPONS

Undoubtedly the most spectacular new weapon was the five-inch High Velocity Aerial Rocket (HVAR), which was issued to composite squadrons in the Atlantic at the end of 1943. Early US Army Air Force 'bazooka' type launchers were tested for possible navy use in the spring of that year, but their low velocity and the weight of the tubular launcher were deemed unsuitable. That summer a British rocket was tested on Avengers, using a rail-type launcher. But shortly the US Navy's Bureau of Ordnance and California Institute of Technology produced the HVAR, fired from 'zero length' rails which reduced weight. TBM-3s came from the factory with zero-length rails and radar sets as standard equipment, which made them ideal for ASW work. The rockets were issued to units in December and were first employed in combat by TBMs from *Block Island* in January 1944.

HVARs were an immediate success. With three-four under each wing, they gave an Avenger more than the broadside of a destroyer. Superior range and penetration made them ideally suited for attacking heavily-armed U-boats, as the attack did not have to be pressed as close as a bomb run. Usually, ASW aircraft carried four HVARs with high-explosive warheads and four with solid heads for penetration.

An effective range of 400 yards was demonstrated against both seaborne and land targets, and the carrier tactical manual specified rocket use against 'small individual targets such as fuel tanks, ammunition dumps, revetted planes, gun emplacements, small buildings, etc. Gun positions in the side of a hill, difficult to hit by a bomb, are suitable targets for rockets'. Aviators agreed. One TBM pilot, after first firing HVARs against Japanese island targets, proclaimed them 'the greatest thing since the nickel cigar.'

Intimately related to ASW weapons was the sonobuoy, available in June 1943. This expendable listening device could be dropped from an Avenger to help track a submarine. Consisting of a hydrophone for detecting underwater noises and a radio transmitter for relaying sounds to the aircraft, it featured prominently in the demise of many subs.

Aerial mines were employed by TBFs or TBMs only once on a large scale. The event occurred during a fast carrier strike by TF-58 against the Palau Islands at the end of March 1944. The Avengers of VT-2,- 8 and -16 laid their mines close to shore in order to bottle up numerous Japanese ships, thus preventing them from leaving anchorage. But it was risky business, as the Avengers had to fly low, predictable patterns within range of shore-based AA guns. Subsequently, mine sowing was done mainly by long-range patrol aircraft or USAAF heavy bombers.

AVENGER AIR-TO-AIR

Thirty US Navy Avenger units were credited with at least 68 aerial victories. Seven of the squadrons were based on escort carriers, and some flew combat missions both ashore and afloat. Top scores were:

Unit		
VT-10	*Enterprise*	7
VT-9	*Essex, Lexington*	6
VT-11	*Guadalcanal, Hornet*	5.5
VT-8	*Guadalcanal, Bunker Hill*	5
VTN-90	*Enterprise*	5
VT-18	*Intrepid*	4
VT-6	*Enterprise*	3
VT-12	*Saratoga*	3
VT-17	*Bunker Hill*	3
VT-32	*Langley*	3

Pilots

Lt C E Henderson	VT-10 and VT(N)-90	3
Lt(jg) C R Largess	VT(N)-90	2
LtCdr J L Phillips	VT-6	2
Lt(jg) J H Drew	VT-32	2

Gunners

ARM3/c G L Hicks	VT-8	2
AMS2/c R B Holgrin	VT-10	2

Three Marine Corps Avenger squadrons claimed 20.5 shootdowns. No leatherneck pilots or gunners gained multiple victories.

VMTB-143	9.5
VMTB-232	6
VMSB-131	5

'Mr Night Attack' was Cdr William I Martin, who commanded VT-10 and Night Air Group 90 aboard *Enterprise* in 1944-45. As a lieutenant (junior grade) he wrote the first instrument flying manual for carrier aviators before the war. Beginning in 1943, his pioneering work in the development of low-level, radar-directed nocturnal bombing proved highly successful, and led to affiliated work involving carrier aviation's earliest electronic countermeasures programme. (*Author's collection*)

The most successful Avenger pilot against enemy aircraft was Lt(jg) Charles English Henderson III, a cheerfully aggressive aviator who turned his lumbering 'Turkey' into a formidable nightfighters. In two combat deployments – VT-10 in 1943-44 and VT(N)-90 in 1945 – the pilot was credited with three confirmed victories and one probable.

Henderson's remarkable record was gained in eight encounters with hostile or unidentified aircraft, both day and night. He survived his first aerial combat – a day mission over Truk Atoll in February 1944 – despite drawing the attention of a Zero pilot, who made five firing passes at Henderson's TBF. By careful timing and extraordinary manoeuvring, Henderson ran the A6M5 pilot out of ammunition, who then departed with a sporting dip of his wings!

In his next encounter, searching for the enemy fleet off Saipan on 18 June, Henderson surprised an Aichi E13A 'Jake' floatplane. He used cloud cover to approach to minimum range and exploded it with 17 rounds of .50-cal. Apparently, the claim was not processed, but two days later Henderson downed a Nakajima B6N 'Jill' scout-bomber.

On the night of 19 March 1945, Henderson's radar operator vectored him onto a multi-engine aircraft at 12,000 ft over Bungo Strait;

'It was a dirty night, with light cloud and misty rain, shortly before dawn. Slowly, we edged closer, and I charged both wing guns. At 300 yards we couldn't see a thing. Then a giant tail emerged, like a spectre.

Lt(jg) Charles English Henderson III aboard *Enterprise* in 1944. Flying consecutive combat tours with VT-10 and VT(N)-90, Henderson established a rare reputation in torpedo squadrons by shooting down at least three, and probably four, Japanese aircraft. Ironically, his VT(N)-90 gunner was Merle Henderson (*Author's collection*)

Then the glow of four engines as I closed in tight formation. An 'Emily'! We had hit the jackpot! I locked my port wing behind his starboard outboard engine and fired. He reacted instantly, turning, weaving, twisting and diving. Grimly, I hung on, flying wing, holding my port gun directly behind his engine nacelle. Time stood still – was endless – was nothing. He strove to shake me off; I clung tenaciously.

'Then I saw the water. We had dropped 12,000 ft. After all our preparations and struggle, we had failed. Better to ram and chop up his tail with my prop. Suddenly I comprehended the *kamikaze* spirit.

'And then a sparkle of flame. I squeezed a long burst, perhaps my last. A larger flame, a fire. Swiftly I pulled up and away from a ball of fire, an immense explosion. Awed in spite of ourselves, we viewed the pyre and flames high in the sky.'

Before dawn on 13 May, Henderson had two combats. He claimed a Kawanishi N1K 'George' as a probable, then chased an A6M2-N Rufe float fighter, and 'after a long dogfight, I managed to turn inside him thanks to wheels and flaps down. He plunged into the sea.'

Eventually, 'Hotshot Charlie' Henderson settled in Australia, living on a large cattle station, where he spent part of his 'retirement' teaching one of his daughters to become a competitive aerobatic pilot.

LOSSES

Avenger losses mounted disproportionately after 1942, reaching what would have been considered insupportable figures for many aircraft. However, because nearly 10,000 TBFs/TBMs were built from 1942 to 1945, the large numbers of actual losses (including write-offs or retirement of 'war weary' airframes) only amounted to about 25 per cent of total production, based solely on US Navy and Marine usage.

From about 100 losses in 1942, with combat limited almost exclusively to the Guadalcanal campaign of late that year, combined attrition nearly tripled to 270 in 1943. The peak wastage that year was 67 in November, which included both Rabaul strikes (18 destroyed) and all 12 of VC-39's TBFs aboard the escort carrier *Liscombe Bay*, torpedoed by a Japanese submarine in the Marshall Islands.

Losses from all causes skyrocketed more than 400 per cent in 1944, reaching 1071, with a peak of 127 in June. The latter figure was no surprise, considering the intensity of operations worldwide. *Block Island*, the only US carrier sunk in the Atlantic, took 11 TBMs to the bottom on 1 June, with 13 more lost chasing U-boats that month. Meanwhile, TF-58 operations off Saipan cost nearly 40 TBFs/TBMs on the 20th alone. Even that figure was eclipsed during the climax at Leyte Gulf, with 54 Avengers lost to all causes on 25 October. Overall, the navy and marines struck off three Avengers a day throughout 1944.

The rate of attrition only accelerated in 1945. With 928 TBFs/TBMs shot down, wrecked or retired, the average wastage was four per day, including 174 in June. Of those, 105 were pool aircraft stricken as war-weary or damaged beyond economical repair.

Like the seasoned veteran that it was, the Avenger took everything that the enemy, nature and a hazardous calling could toss at it. And on the last day of the war, the old veteran was still standing, still taking the fight to the enemy, and giving far better than it got.

APPENDICES

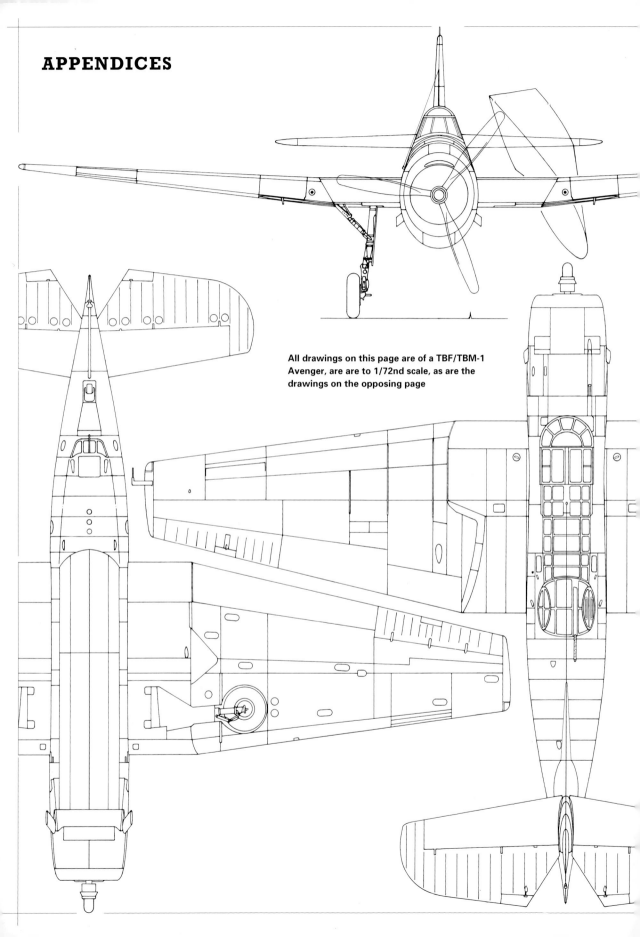

All drawings on this page are of a TBF/TBM-1
Avenger, are are to 1/72nd scale, as are the
drawings on the opposing page

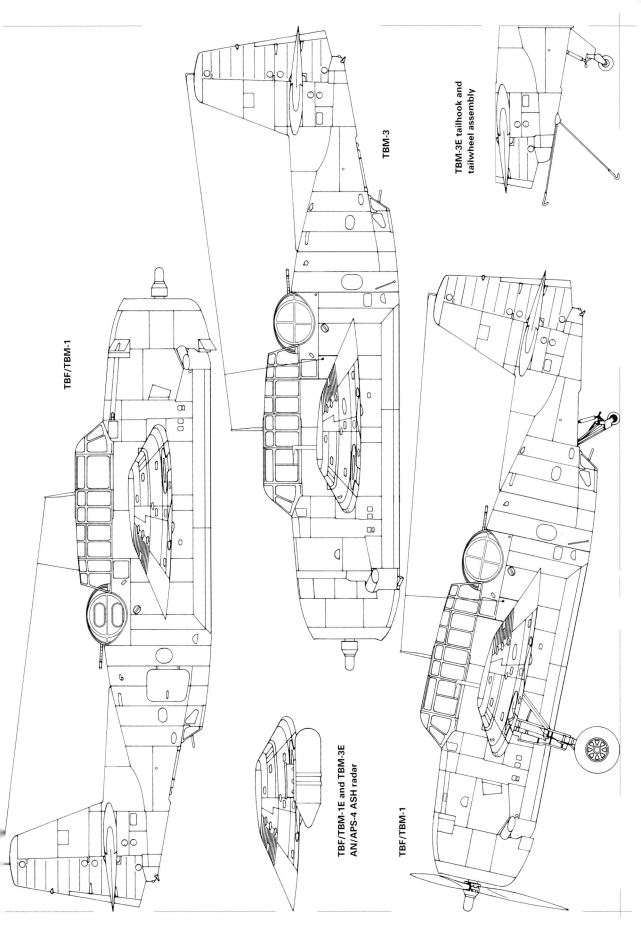

TBM-3

TBM-3E tailhook and tailwheel assembly

TBF/TBM-1

TBF/TBM-1E and TBM-3E
AN/APS-4 ASH radar

TBF/TBM-1

COLOUR PLATES

1
TBF-1C White 95 of VT-2, USS *Hornet* (CV 12), August 1944

As Air Group 2 approached the end of its long deployment aboard the second *Hornet*, this TBF had earned an unusual record. Displayed on the starboard side were 53 bombs for strike missions and three silhouettes indicating torpedo attacks against Japanese ships. At this phase of the war, it was an unusually high proportion of torpedo to bombing missions. Torpedo Two participated in the Philippine Sea battle, and undoubtedly one of the aircraft's 'torpecker' runs occurred during the strike on the Japanese fleet on the evening of 20 June 1944.

2
TBF-1C White 3 of VT-7, USS *Hancock* (CV 19), late 1944

Variously described as a horse shoe or the omega sign, *Hancock*'s Air Group 7 bore this distinctive emblem during its combat deployment from October 1944 to January 1945. VT-7 was unusual in placing the aircraft number on the access panel behind the engine cowling, rather than farther forward on the nose.

3
TBF-1 White 64 of VT-8, USS *Saratoga* (CV 3), September 1942

The original TBF squadron, Torpedo Eight rebounded from its ill-fated Midway debut to become one of the notable Avenger units. Reorganised in Hawaii during June 1942, the squadron boarded *Saratoga* in time for the Guadalcanal landings in August, and participated in the carrier battle that same month. This TBF-1 bears typical 1942 colours – blue-grey over medium grey below. The previous squadron letters (8-T-1, for instance) has been replaced by a generic fuselage number.

4
TBM-3 White 22 of VC-8, USS *Nehenta Bay* (CVE 74), February 1945

Probably the most distinctive of all escort carrier markings was *Nehenta Bay*'s inverted arrow head. Embarking in CVE-74 in February, VC-8 was directly involved in the Iwo Jima and Okinawa operations. That summer the emblematic and geometric tail markings were replaced by a highly systematic series of stripes and bands on wings and tails, which enabled a knowledgeable observer to determine the CVE group to which the unit was assigned, and within the group the specific ship, and therefore squadron. However, the system had not been in use anywhere near long enough for sailors or airmen in the frontline to effectively learn the nuances before the end of hostilities saw many units disbanded and carriers decommissioned.

5
TBM-1C White B1 of VC-10, flown by unit CO, Lt Cdr E J Huxtable, USS *Gambier Bay* (CVE 73), October 1944

Lt Cdr Edward J Huxtable, a former dive-bomber pilot, formed VC-10 and led it through two combat deployments. The only squadron ever assigned to *Gambier Bay*, VC-10 remained with the ship until it sunk off Samar in the Battle of Leyte Gulf on 25 October 1944. The squadron was unusual in the number of TBMs and FMs that displayed nose art, with the CO's aircraft leading by example. 'Hux's' B1 bore an inspection panel on the port side with no fewer than five artfully-rendered small 'Petty girls' in various poses. Despite having lost his ship and all of his aircraft with the sinking of Gambier Bay, Huxtable reformed the squadron in 1945 and returned to the Pacific shortly before VJ-Day.

6
TBF-1 White T-1 of VT-10, flown by unit CO, Lt Cdr W I Martin, USS *Enterprise* (CV 6), late 1943

This is one of the most unusual of all Avengers. The combat-experienced Lt Cdr William I Martin wanted more forward-firing guns for his VT-10 TBFs before returning to the Pacific aboard *Enterprise* in late 1943. Therefore, he had his armourers mount .50-cal guns externally on each wingroot, synchronised to fire through the propeller arc. The arrangement, supervised by Grumman technician Ralph Clark, worked satisfactorily, but was not adopted by other aircraft. However, TBF-1Cs had two internal wing-mounted .50-cals as standard equipment. Martin's T-1 has white undersides and the standard two-tone 1942-43 upper surfaces, with a darker than normal rudder. The squadron's unique 'Buzzard Brigade' emblem is displayed forward of the cockpit in a white disk.

7
TBF-1C White 93 of VT-15, USS *Essex* (CV 9), November 1944

This VT-15 aircraft sustained heavy battle damage during a strike against the Philippines in November 1944. The turret gunner was killed in action, and as the TBF was considered damaged beyond economical repair, the gunner was buried at sea, still strapped into his battle station. White 93 was probably a fairly recent arrival in *Essex*, as the chalked ferry number was still visible on the cowling.

8
TBM-3 White 133 of VT-20, USS *Lexington* (CV 16), January 1945

VT-20's squadron markings were unusual for this period, but reflected the growing trend in the Fast Carrier Task Force toward three-digit numbers. This TBM participated in the strike against French Indochina on 12-13 January 1945, marking the first time in nearly three years that Allied surface ships had sailed in the South China Sea.

9

TBM-1C BuNo 46203 White 23 of VC-21, USS *Marcus Island* (CVE 77), August 1944

Composite Squadron 21 flew from the escort carrier *Marcus Island* between August 1944 and February 1945. Named for the small island that was struck by US carrier aeroplanes in early 1942, CVE-77 was heavily involved in the Philippine campaign. A VC-21 Avenger sighted and helped sink a Japanese midget submarine stalking the cruiser reportedly taking Gen Douglas MacArthur's staff to Luzon in January 1945, thereby gaining the appreciation of the supreme commander of the Southwest Pacific Theatre of Operations.

10

TBF-1 Black 22-C-4 of VC-22, USS *Independence* (CVL 22), May 1943

Reflecting the transitional period of US Navy colours, this TBF bears the early combination of the 1943 tri-colour scheme while retaining 1942-43 national insignia. The legend on the fuselage was primarily used in 'Stateside' training and work-ups, being replaced by simpler numerals in the combat area. VC-22 later became VT-22, embarking in *Belleau Wood* and *Independence* for strikes against Baker, Howland, Tarawa, Wake Island and Rabaul.

11

TBF-1C White 9 of VT-9. flown by Lt(jg) Warren Omark, USS *Belleau Wood* (CVL 24), June 1944

Belleau Wood's VT-24 was the only US torpedo squadron to sink an enemy aircraft carrier alone and unassisted. On 20 June a division led by Lt(jg) George Brown attacked IJNS *Hiyo* during the dusk strike known as 'the mission beyond darkness'. Brown and two other pilots launched their torpedoes against the enemy 'flattop' and scored at least one, possibly two hits (Japanese records are contradictory). *Hiyo* was unable to control her damage and sank that night, observed by Brown's two aircrewmen, who had bailed out when his Avenger caught fire. Brown failed to return to the task force and was lost at sea. His section leader was Lt(jg) Warren Omark, whose assigned aircraft was No 9, although he is uncertain whether he flew that Avenger on 20 June.

12

TBF-1 Black 26-GS-10 of VGS-26, USS *Charger* (CVE 30), late 1942

Escort Scouting Squadron 26 was one of three TBF units supporting the American landings in French Morocco during November 1942. The Avenger is painted in typical early war colours – blue-grey upper and medium grey undersurfaces, with the national insignia in six positions. Many naval aircraft supporting Operation *Torch* retained their 'Stateside' markings, in contrast to later practise which emphasised security. The other notable feature of *Torch* markings was an insignia yellow border around the fuselage star, not yet applied to this *Charger* aircraft. VGS-26 flew from USS *Sangamon* during Operation *Torch*.

13

TBF-1C White 7 of VT-31, USS *Cabot* (CVL 28), July 1944

Torpedo Squadron 31's marking was the rear half of the rudder painted white against the tri-colour blue scheme. Embarking in the light carrier *Cabot* in January 1944, the unit saw extensive combat over the next eight months, with operations against the Marshalls, Carolines, Marianas and Palaus, as well as preliminary strikes against the Philippines. The *Cabot* cruise ended in September 1944, but Air Group 31 returned to the Western Pacific in the summer of 1945, completing VJ-Day missions from *Cabot's* sister CVL, *Belleau Wood*.

14

TBM-3E White 27 of VT-34, USS *Monterey* (CVL 26), July 1945

An excellent example of late-war carrier markings, this Avenger's overall gloss blue colour scheme vividly sets off the standard as well as non-regulation markings. In July 1945 the previous geometric air group identifiers were replaced with letters, *Monterey* drawing 'C'. Assigned a CVE air group rather than the usual composite squadron, the ship operated VT-34, whose number 27 aircraft displayed 18 white bombs as mission markers in addition to the ever-popular Vargas pin-up girl in a suitably sultry pose – just the thing to keep up aviators' and sailors' morale as VJ-Day approached.

15

TBM-1D White 22 of VT(N)-41, USS *Independence* (CVL 22), October 1944

While many F6F-3E/N 'bat teams' had two Avengers attached, the first Avenger squadron dedicated to night attack was VT(N)-41 in Lt Cdr Turner F Caldwell's Night Air Group 41. Deployed in the light carrier *Independence* in 1944-45, VT(N)-41 played a significant role in the Battle of Leyte Gulf. On the night of 24-25 October, Lt W R Taylor's Avengers tracked Vice Adm Kurita's powerful battleship and cruiser force through San Bernardino Strait, providing valuable intelligence that corrected the impression that Kurita had withdrawn westward earlier in the day. However, VT(N)-41's information was not acted upon by Adm W F Halsey's Third Fleet staff, and Kurita emerged into Leyte Gulf early on the 25th, resulting in the lopsided Battle off Samar.

16

TBM-1C Black 16 of VC-42, USS *Bogue* (CVE 9), July 1944

The Atlantic colour scheme was arguably the most attractive applied to any naval aircraft of World War 2. Insignia white overall, with sea grey applied to most of the upper surfaces, was optimised for the hazy conditions often found in northern waters. VC-42 flew from five CVEs, with Atlantic combat cruises in *Croatan* and *Bogue* in 1944, and Pacific operations aboard *Corregidor* in 1945. This aircraft (number 16) was destroyed with three others when a *Bogue* TBF suffered hook failure and crashed through the barriers. In honour of the event, the hapless pilot received a makeshift Iron Cross from his shipmates!

17
TBM-1C White 51-T-8 of VT-51, USS *San Jacinto* (CVL 30), February 1944
This Avenger logged a barrier engagement during VT-51 work-ups aboard *San Jacinto* in February 1944. Still in American waters, the aircraft retained its full identification as per prewar practise. Upon deploying to the Pacific war zone, Air Group 51's Avengers and Hellcats were identified with a white X on the rudder, flying combat missions from 'San Jac' between May and November 1944. It was one of only a handful of fast carrier air group markings based on a letter prior to the replacement of geometric symbols with alphabet-based ship identification in mid-1945.

18
TBF-1C Black 58-C-26 *Len-Sharon* of VC-58, USS *Block Island* (CVE 21), January 1944
The crew of this aircraft participated in the US Navy's first rocket attack against a submarine. On 11 January 1944, Lt(jg) L L McFord, with his crewmen, ARM3/c C Gertsch and AMM2/c WH Ryder, sighted the surfaced U-758. Another TBF, flown by Lt(jg) W D Seeley, also attacked, inflicting damage that forced the U-boat to return to base. VC-58 was eventually credited with three U-boat kills while deployed aboard *Guadalcanal* and *Wake Island*. *Len-Sharon* is unusual in apparently being insignia white overall, without the grey portion of the ETO colour scheme.

19
TBF-1C White N19 of VC-63, USS *Natoma Bay* (CVE 62), February 1944
Several escort carrier groups used alpha-numeric designators for their aircraft, including those of *Natoma Bay* in early 1944. VC-63's Avengers and Wildcats displayed N prefixes in addition to the simple vertical stripe parallel to the rudder hinge line. Mixing letter identifications with geometric symbols was unusual, but removed all room for doubt as to which ship or squadron the aircraft belonged. VC-63 flew from *Natoma Bay* during the first seven months of 1944 – an unusually long deployment, spanning the Marshalls, New Ireland and Hollandia (New Guinea) strikes.

20
TBM-3 White 113 of VT-82, USS *Bennington* (CV 20), February 1945
This Avenger was subject of one of the most dramatic aircraft photos of World War 2. Heavy flak damage resulted in the loss of nearly half the port wing, in addition to a five-foot section of the fuse-lage decking immediately aft of the turret. However, the VT-82 pilot skilfully retained control of his doomed TBM long enough to make a successful water landing. Standard early 1945 colours and markings were gloss blue overall with the *Bennington* 'Christmas tree', or arrowhead, repeated on the upper starboard wing, overlapping the aileron.

21
TBM-3 White 301 of VT-84, USS *Bunker Hill* (CV 17), February 1945
Another variation on an arrow for a 'G symbol' was the vertical emblem of Air Group 84 aboard the veteran *Essex*-class ship *Bunker Hill* in early 1945. This tri-colour TBM also had the symbol on the upper starboard wing, measuring nearly full chord between the aileron and leading edge. The most distinctive feature was the yellow nose band, a special recognition measure applied for the first Tokyo strikes in February and retained at least until March. The individual aircraft number, painted in small white figures on the vertical stabiliser, was repeated in black on the cowling.

22
TBM-3 White 121 of VT-88, USS *Yorktown* (CV 10), August 1945
The RR tail code replaced *Yorktown's* previous air group emblem – a diagonally-aligned segment of the tail surfaces – in June 1945. At that time most fast carrier air groups switched to one- or two-letter codes, although a few retained geometric symbols until the end of hostilities. VT-88 participated in strikes against the Japanese Home Islands during July and August, its most notable attacks being flown against heavy surface units moored in Kure Harbour.

23
TBM-3D White/Black 68 of VT(N)-90, USS *Enterprise* (CV 6), early 1945
'The Big E' pioneered night strike operations in carrier warfare, beginning with VT-10's Truk raid in February 1944. Less than a year later the ship was back with a full-time night air group under the same innovator, Cdr William I Martin. The TBM-3Ds had the outline arrow emblem, which often was partly or wholly obscured with blue or grey paint to reduce contrast. However, some aircrew felt that the reduced visibility markings were unnecessary owing to the near absence of Japanese nightfighters by that stage of the war.

24
TBM-3 White 90 of VC-96, USS *Rudyerd Bay* (CVE 81), April 1945
The grid, or 'tic-tac-toe', emblem appeared on the tails of VC-96 Avengers and Wildcats bearing both tri-colour and gloss blue schemes. Engaged in the latter stages of the Western Pacific campaign, *Rudyerd Bay* escorted the vital at-sea replenishment group that sustained the fast carriers of Task Force 38 from March to July 1945. That four-

month period involved the Okinawa campaign, as well as strikes against the Japanese home islands.

25

TBM-3 White 32 of VC-97, USS *Makassar Strait* (CVE 91), March 1945

The fish hook emblem of *Makassar Strait* was certainly appropriate for VC-97 Avengers, whose duties included anti-submarine patrols during the ship's February-May 1945 deployment. The squadron's aircraft conducted ASW and combat air patrols for the fast carrier replenishment group during the Iwo Jima operation, then provided close air support at Okinawa. However, by that time the Japanese submarine force had largely been negated, and relatively few allied warships were attacked – let alone sunk – by conventional submarines.

26

TBM-3 Yellow 57 of VMTB-132, USS *Cape Gloucester* (CVE 109), July 1945

Typical of most escort carrier markings after June 1945, this Marine Corps TBM displays the system of white and yellow stripes, or bands, which identified the individual carrier and its task group. Led by Capt Henry Hise, VMTB-132 belonged to Marine Carrier Air Group Four, which also included the Corsairs of VMF-351 aboard *Cape Gloucester*. The Avengers participated briefly in the Okinawa campaign, then operated in the East China Sea, undertaking strikes along the Asian mainland.

27

TBM-3 White 53 of VMTB-233, USS *Block Island* (CVE 106), May 1945

Rare among Marine Corps TBM units, VMTB-233 was one of only four 'Leatherneck' Avenger squadrons carrier based during 1945. Boarding the second USS *Block Island* in March, the squadron comprised half of Marine Carrier Air Group One, joined by the FG-1D Corsairs and F6F-5N/P Hellcats of VMF-511. *Block Island* aviators supported infantry on Okinawa from May, and also conducted strike operations elsewhere in the Ryukyus. The air group identification system was entirely symbolic and logical – a white block with the black letter I!

28

TBF-1C Yellow E16 of an unidentified Operational Training Unit, USS *Mission Bay* (CVE 59), November 1943

Engaged in Atlantic carrier qualification trials aboard the escort carrier *Mission Bay*, this TBF-1C bore unusual markings for late 1943. The overall tri-colour scheme is highlighted by the Insignia Red border around the national emblem, a short-lived variation replaced by the pure Insignia Blue background in January 1944. The large 'E16' overpainted on the fuselage 'star-and-bars' was rendered in large yellow figures, perhaps to discourage freshly-taught naval aviators from indulging in prohibited low flying!

29

Avenger II JZ466 White 380 of No 848 Sqn, HMS *Formidable* (67), August 1945

The British Pacific Fleet (BPF) operated as a task group of the US Third Fleet during the latter part of the Pacific war, flying missions over Japan proper. This aircraft's overall scheme is temperate maritime, with light grey undersurfaces – the demarcation line runs slightly more than halfway up the side of the cowling. BPF roundels are carried in four positions, and the ship's distinctive 'X' and the side number are rendered in white. Finally, the serial JZ466 is lettered in black on the dorsal strake.

30

Avenger I JZ114 of No 848 Sqn, HMS *Formidable* (67), August 1945

Due to the proven reliability of their lend-lease types, the Fleet Air Arm kept their aircraft in front-line service far longer between major overhauls than their American allies. Hence, No 848 Sqn could be found operating a 'mixed bag' of Avenger Is and IIs during the final stages of the Pacific war.

31

Avenger II Red Q of No 853 Sqn, HMS *Queen*, April 1945

The contrast of maritime slate grey and sea green colours over insignia white is evident in this aircraft operating from *Queen* in the spring of 1945. Unusual is the repetition of the fuselage cockade, with the narrow white centre ring, on the wings in place of the blue and red variety. 'Royal Navy' is stencilled in white on the dorsal strake leading to the vertical fin, with the serial number below. As with most FAA Avengers, the fuselage observer's blister is more prominent than on USN aircraft. *Queen* launched several strikes into Scandinavian waters in the last months of the European war.

32

Tarpon I FN910 White 4F of No 846 Sqn, Macrihanish, Scotland, December 1943

Amongst the second batch of Tarpon Is delivered to the British in the autumn of 1943, this aircraft was issued to No 846 Sqn after the unit had flown off HMS *Ravager* and taken up residence in Scotland. It was heavily used during the subsequent work-up period, being photographed in colour by the legendary Charles E Brown whilst participating in a press day that served to introduce the new type to the British public – No 846 Sqn was the first unit to operate the Tarpon I in home waters.

33

Avenger I JZ159 Red 2F/Black 59 of No 852 Sqn, HMS *Nabob*, early 1944

The Tarpon I became the Avenger I through a simple name change on 13 January 1944, this profile showing No 852 Sqn's JZ159 at around the time of the swap. The repetition of part of the aircraft's serial on the lower cowling gives it a modicum of individuality, and a number of other aircraft assigned to Home Fleet carriers at around this period also utilised a similar marking. JZ159 saw much action with No 852 Sqn whilst embarked on the Canadian-manned carrier *Nabob* between 11 February and 6 April 1944, flying anti-shipping strikes and parachute mine-laying sorties off the Norwegian coast.

35
Avenger II JZ525 White P1X of No 849 Sqn, HMS *Victorious* (38), January 1945
Amongst the first Fleet Air Arm squadrons established in the USA to fly the Tarpon I in mid-1943, No 849 Sqn initially served with the Home Fleet and from coastal bases in the UK. However, in September 1944 it embarked on HMS *Rajah* and headed east to bolster the Allied war effort against the Japanese. By now equipped with Avenger IIs, the unit became part of No 2 Naval Strike Wing (with fellow Avenger II operators No 820 Sqn) aboard HMS *Victorious* on 10 December 1944, and remained with the vessel until it returned to the UK in October 1945. During the final eight months of the war in the Pacific, the unit played a key role in numerous actions involving the BPF, striking at targets ranging from the Sumatran oil refineries to the Sakishima Islands and Formosa, and finally the Japanese mainland around Tokyo. This aircraft was a participant in the first raids flown against the huge refineries at Pangkalan, Brandon and Palembang, in the East Indies, which were staged in January 1945. Significant damage was caused to the targets by the British Avengers.

35
TBF-1C NZ2506 White E of No 30 Sqn, Piva, early 1944
Unlike the Fleet Air Arm, the Royal New Zealand Air Force chose not to bother repainting the 48 Avengers supplied to them from US Navy stocks in late 1943. They did, however, mark them up with the two-tone blue, white and yellow roundel and thin red, white and blue rudder flash synonymous with all RNZAF combat aircraft in the Pacific theatre. Initially, No 30 Sqn also flirted with single letter codes as well, although these were soon dropped when it was found that they interfered with the white recognition bars applied on either side of the roundel. This aircraft was based at Piva, Bougainville, in the spring of 1944.

36
TBF-1C NZ2518 White 518 of No 30 Sqn, flown by Flt Lt Fred Ladd, Piva, May 1944
Undoubtedly the most famous of all Kiwi TBFs, NZ2518 was christened PLONKY in honour of its teetotalling pilot, Flt Lt Fred Ladd. The nose art just aft of the aircraft's cowling featured a winged beer barrel leaving its contents trailing in its wake through an ajar tap. Known even to 'Tokyo Rose', who once referred to it in her broadcast as 'Plocky', the aircraft saw much action from Piva in the first half of 1944. Damaged at least twice in combat (once by its own ordnance, which was dropped at too low an altitude), it was passed on to No 31 Sqn on 25 May 1944 and lost in action – along with its three-man crew – just 11 days later when struck down by ground fire.

BIBLIOGRAPHY

Dresser, James. *Escort Carriers and Air Unit Markings During WW II in the Pacific.* privately published, 1980
Franks, Norman, and Eric Zimmerman. *U-Boat versus Aircraft.* Grub Street, 1998
Lambert, John W. *Wildcats Over Casablanca, November 1942.* Phalanx, 1992
Lovisolo, Lois. *Grumman Aircraft Data from 1930.* Grumman, 1993.
Lundstrom, John B. *The First Team and the Guadalcanal Campaign.* Naval Institute Press, 1994.
Lovisolo, Lois. *Grumman Aircraft Data.* Grumman Aerospace, 1993.
Sturdivant, Ray. *British Naval Aviation: the Fleet Air Arm 1917-1990.* Naval Institute Press, 1990
Tillman, Barrett. *Avenger at War.* Ian Allan Ltd, 1979
Tillman, Barrett. 'Leyte Plus Fifty', *The Hook*, Fall 1994.
Tillman, Barrett. 'The CVE Program', *The Hook*, Winter 1986
US Navy. *Current Tactical Orders and Doctrine, US Fleet, USF 74B.* November 1944
Wagner, Ray. *American Combat Planes.* Doubleday, 1968.